Walk the Plank
Winning the Game of Life on 4th Down

Doug Plank
with Lee Witt

ISBN: 978-1-64719-266-2

Published by BookLocker.com, Inc., St. Petersburg, Florida.

Printed on acid-free paper.

BookLocker.com, Inc.
2021

First Edition

Library of Congress Cataloguing in Publication Data
Plank, Doug and Witt, Lee
Walk the Plank: Winning the Game of Life on 4th Down by Doug Plank with Lee Witt
Library of Congress Control Number: 2020925152

To Nancy,

Who knew that an errant snowball could lead to lifelong love?
Thank you for always being there.

And for Andrea and Michael,

The legacy will someday be yours.

CONTENTS

Foreword vii

A Note About Doug Plank ix

SECTION ONE: Controlling the Mind 1

    Chapter One - Use Your Life: Your Genetic Potential Awaits 1
    Chapter Two – Bring Your "A" Game: 100% All the Time 13

SECTION TWO: Communication and Influence 67

    Chapter Three – Deliver the Message: An Arrow Straight to the Heart 67
    Chapter Four – Control the Environment: Presence, Power and Warmth 93

SECTION THREE: Making the Last Thing You Ever Do Your Greatest 97

    Chapter Five – Attack to the Very End 97

Appendix A: VISION AND PLANNING EXERCISE 117

Appendix B: YOUR "A" GAME 119

Appendix C: The "46 Attack Mindset" Questions 121

Appendix D: The 46 Bullet Point Summary 123

SPECIAL BONUS APPENDIX E: SKILLS THAT DO NOT TAKE TALENT! 127

ACKNOWLEDGEMENTS 129

DOUG PLANK BIOGRAPHY 131

Foreword

The Chicago Bears are one of the oldest and most storied franchises in all of professional football. No other team has had so many great players and so many incredible characters. From Red Grange, Bronko Nagurski and Sid Luckman to Dick Butkus, Gale Sayers and Walter Payton, this team's legacy has always been one of competitive excellence.

Having won championships as both a Chicago Bear player and coach, I was fortunate to have played with and coached many of the Bear greats. One of my favorites was Doug Plank. Doug was one of the best players I ever had – tough as nails – and I was honored when asked to write the foreword to his book.

When I took the head coaching job in Chicago, Doug had already established himself as one of the hardest hitters in the game. His ability to accelerate from his safety position to the point of impact on a ball carrier was unmatched. But most of all, I loved that Doug gave 100% in every practice and every game. That's all you can ask from a player. Doug played with both brains and brawn. He wasn't the biggest guy, but he got everything he could out of his body and mind. He was always prepared, and he went all-out every time. That's what has made him successful as a player, coach, businessman and broadcaster.

This book gives you a glimpse into the mentality that has made Doug special. He shares his successes, failures and the keys that can enable any person to get the most from his or her God-given ability. These lessons can help anyone to reach their ultimate potential. I hope you will take his lessons to heart.

Mike Ditka

A Note About Doug Plank

Doug Plank is the poster boy for anyone who was ever told that they were too small, too slow, or too inexperienced to succeed. His exceptional career in the National Football League is testimony that anyone can make their capabilities exceed their limitations. Through hard work, discipline, preparation and the ability to suppress his own survival instincts, Doug Plank overcame all obstacles to reach the upper limits of his genetic potential.

This is not just another motivational self-help book – although you will certainly be motivated. This book takes you beyond motivation into the psyche of a man who "willed" himself to excellence through a relentless desire to get the most out of himself. He said "Yes" to every opportunity and in so doing, he became an example to millions when his Chicago Bear defensive coach, Buddy Ryan, named the famous "46 Bear defense" after him and his number.

To those who know football, he is a legend. True Chicago Bear fans were crestfallen that Doug retired just two seasons before they won the 1986 Super Bowl. But his toughness, grit and spirit lived through that team and the famous "take no prisoners" 46 defense was instrumental in their Super Bowl success.

When Doug was on the football field, no one was spared. He played with a headfirst reckless abandon that has influenced football rule changes to this day. Watching him was like watching an unguided missile that would launch into the fray taking out opponents, teammates and anyone in the way. Collateral damage was a given. His ability to control his mind and take this aggressive approach to football has also propelled him to succeed in both business and life.

And it's this approach that can take you, at any age and in any profession, to the top of your chosen field.

Doug calls this approach, "The 46 Attack Mindset." But this approach comes with a caution. There is a cost to the kind of success that Doug has enjoyed. Game after game Doug made devastating hits, sacrificing his body to succeed. You will have to make sacrifices as well to succeed at the highest level of whatever game you're in. In any field of endeavor, there is a price to pay. That's just how it works.

Doug Plank willingly paid that price. He recognizes the sacrifices and his shoulders, hips and knees remind him of those sacrifices every day. But the beauty of Doug Plank is that he wouldn't change a thing. He still loves the game and he values his time in it, as a player, a coach, and a broadcaster. Even with bionic body parts, there are no regrets.

In this book, you will learn how to adopt the 100% all out, old school attitude that characterizes the "46 Attack Mindset." Doug's willingness to take on every challenge head-on is what took him from a small town in Western Pennsylvania to unprecedented levels of success in sports and business. Adopting this mindset will enable you to reach the upper limits of your genetic potential as well.

SECTION ONE: Controlling the Mind

Chapter One - Use Your Life: Your Genetic Potential Awaits

*Try running into a wall. A normal person will slow down at the last moment—a hitter will accelerate. When people say I was great in my day, I say, no, I was just able to control my mind for those few seconds before impact. I never slowed down. I sped up. That's what makes a hitter. Not size, not speed. **It's the ability to suppress your survival instincts.***

Doug Plank

Why would anyone choose to suppress their survival instincts? After all, those instincts exist for a reason.

They exist to keep you safe, to keep you alive.

Suppressing your survival instincts seems rather extreme, doesn't it? What could possibly be worth dying for? What could you want so badly that you would risk death or extreme injury?

For most reasonable people, the answer is fairly obvious and completely logical…nothing. It is very reasonable to say and understand that really nothing is worth dying for.

When you list what a person might be capable of accomplishing, such as becoming a professional athlete, an outstanding musician, or a successful entrepreneur, does any of it actually seem like something you'd be willing to die for?

In reality…

It all is.

Why?

Because you are going to die anyway!

It's only a matter of when. At what point will you decide that life is worth playing at 100% full throttle? A year from now? A month? A week?

You don't have to wait any longer…

As long as you have a single breath left you are still in the game. Your life matters and you can seize this opportunity. No matter what your circumstances, you still have the power of choice.

The real question is, what price are you willing to pay?

Everything comes with a price.

This book is an opportunity to explore how much you are willing to pay in order to accomplish your goals. It will serve as your manual on how to move forward in the face of any obstacle. You will be exploring a philosophy I call "The 46 Attack Mindset."

This mindset is not a gimmick nor is it some "flavor of the day" motivation-speak.

This mindset is a systematic, aggressive approach to life. It encourages you to grow in such a way that *the last thing you ever do can be the greatest thing you ever do*. It captures the 100% all-out effort and aggression that was the hallmark of the famous Chicago Bear 46 defense. That's why it's called the "46 Attack Mindset."

For a moment, stop and think about what it means to "suppress your survival instincts." It's essentially where heroism comes from.

Think of the soldiers in battle who run towards enemy fire.

Think of firefighters who willingly run into the flames.

Think of police officers who face uncertain dangers every day.

The men and women who perform these tasks are heroes who have learned to suppress their survival instincts long enough to perform the jobs that need to be done.

As you will discover, these heroes have learned something very important. They have learned the same thing that those who accomplish great things have discovered.

They have discovered that the world's greatest accomplishments have never come from reasonable people. They have always come from *unreasonable* people.

This book is about learning how to become *unreasonable*.

———

Just what are we capable of? In truth, none of us actually know. We all have different talents, strengths and weaknesses. But too often, we think success simply means not failing. We too often play not to lose instead of playing to win. So we set our goals too low, sell ourselves short, and underachieve. That's why it's important to make the decision to work towards reaching the upper limits of our genetic potential, whatever that potential is. Working to be the best that we can be and making our capabilities exceed our limitations is foundational to the "46 Attack Mindset."

For example, I'm not genetically designed to be six feet five inches tall. That was never going to happen and it wasn't something I could control. I was genetically programmed to be about 6 feet tall.

But what I did with that programmed height was up to me. That I *could* control. So I lifted weights, ran wind sprints, shocked my system, overcame pain and injury and used the intelligence I was given to make myself the best I could possibly be. Using every ounce of my potential was the only way I could have ever competed in the National Football League.

And yes, there were limits to how strong I could get and how fast I could run. But I didn't know what those limits were.

So I took action.

Whether in sports or life, everything begins with action. Without action you remain stagnant. The beauty of the famous Chicago Bear 46 defense was in its innovative approach to taking action. Usually, defenses would "read and react." They would base what they did on whatever the offense was doing.

The 46 defense was different. We acted first and forced the offense to react to us. It was "act, read and react." We took action immediately and that aggressive style was instrumental to our success. We focused on our strengths and what we did well – and we always got off first.

We can do the same in life and business. We can be first to the market with our products. We can be the first to implement the best customer service. We can be the best at caring for our employees and each other. We can be proactive in every aspect of our business.

None of us know our limits until we take massive action towards reaching our potential. It seems obvious that action begets results yet how many people refuse to even take that first step. And those who begin often never finish. They choose the path of least resistance in order to avoid the necessary sacrifices and pain that lead to great accomplishment. Their entire life is played at a reduced level.

If you are reading this book, I assume you are interested in performing at the highest level of which you are capable. Adopting the "46 Attack Mindset" will provide the quickest route to propelling yourself towards the results you desire. But make no mistake…there will be pain and sacrifice.

—

Winston Churchill said, "How easy it is to do nothing."

What would happen if you did not make any calls today? What if you failed to interact with anyone, on the phone, online or in person?

The "46 Attack Mindset" begins with the premise that being proactive is always better than reactive. Positive action must be a part of your daily life.

You have a choice. You can be a spectator in life watching from the bleachers. Or you can get onto the playing field. This book is for those who want to get into the game. To help you make the choice to be a player, here is an example of a clear and primary distinction that will immediately propel you from spectator to player. This is one of the most profound understandings you can have.

I believe that fundamentally, there are two kinds of people. These people take very different approaches to life. They are:

1. People who move through life thinking about all of the things that are going to happen to them versus,

2. People who spend their time doing what they need to get done.

There are no doubt infinite shades of gray within these two categories. But for the purposes of simplicity and clarity, those shades do not matter. You can examine your life and ask yourself which category you fall under.

Person number one lives from the question, "What is going to happen to me?" Person number two lives from the question, "What do I need to get done?"

Do you see the difference? The first question is passive, reactive and reeks of fear. It locks you into a paralysis of inaction. The second question is proactive and positions you to move through and beyond fear to take action.

Too often, we get stuck in "What's going to happen to me?" During those moments, we feel weak and powerless. We feel trapped in frustration, anger and fear. It's not until we get into "What do I need to get done?" that we begin propelling ourselves towards our target.

These two questions are always lurking somewhere in the background of our lives. Those who adopt the "46 Attack Mindset" ask the second question, "What do I need to get done?" Making this vital distinction immediately puts you into the stance of a player. Under stress and pressure, focusing on what you need to get done drives you towards a positive outcome. And you find yourself building momentum as you continue moving forward. We will revisit this vital distinction periodically throughout the book. It is fundamental to the "46 Attack Mindset."

———

Author Jim Rohn said that there are essentially only two pains in life; the pain of execution or the pain of regret. The pain of execution occurs whenever we take action. Yes, being a player often means that we must make sacrifices, overcome difficulties and exercise daily discipline to either succeed or fail in our chosen pursuit. It can be painful.

But the pain of regret is far worse. The pain of regret is characterized by the failure to act. There are always reasons and excuses for inaction. Usually, it's because we're afraid to fail. Other times, we think we're too tired or there isn't enough time. Sometimes, we just lack the determination required to be a player and finish what we've begun.

It's important to distinguish between these two pains because if we choose the pain of execution, even if we fail, we still have the satisfaction of knowing that we put forth our best effort. We competed. *We were in the game!* This pain can be measured mentally in pounds of effort. But the initial pain fades quickly because we know in our souls that we gave it our best shot.

The pain of regret is another matter. This pain can be measured in tons as it weighs on our conscience due to our own inaction. It dawns on us that we will never know what we missed by sitting on the sidelines. Had we taken action, we might have gone down a completely different path or landed in a different occupation. We might be experiencing an entirely different level of personal happiness. If only…

The worst part of the pain of regret is that, not only does it guarantee failure, it grows with time as we realize that time has passed us by – and time is our most valuable commodity. We only have a certain amount of time on this planet. And time is something we can never recover.

I encourage people to live life as if they only have a short time to accomplish their goals. It is better to treat every day as a sprint rather than a marathon. Certainly, you want to make long term plans. But those long-term plans should be made up of the day-to-day sprints that will ultimately get you there. It is your short-term goals – your sprints – that make up the moments of your life.

Everything in life matters. You are either moving closer to your goals, staying the same, or moving backward. As I get older, I realize that every moment that I'm watching television or reading a newspaper, I'm not accomplishing my dreams.

I've also realized that making progress is mostly a frame of mind. Think about the final days before a trip or vacation. There are a number of things you must get done before leaving. You typically work at a frantic pace. You begin calling, planning, working and accomplishing a long list of items in a very short period of time. These "smart effort sprints" can sometimes lead to unprecedented levels of productivity. With focused intensity, we can get a lot accomplished quickly.

What if we performed at this pace every day? What if we approached every day as if it was fourth down and potentially the last day of our life?

We can.

If we begin each day with a plan, start early and work efficiently, we can do more than we ever imagined. The game of life is really a series of habits. When we ingrain *productive* daily habits into our lifestyle, our level of performance rises accordingly. Time becomes an ally instead of our enemy.

Make time your ally. Commit to using this present moment. No matter how old you are, how rich or poor, or whatever circumstances you find yourself in, you can begin again. Right now.

Make the choice right now to get off the bleachers and into the game. It doesn't matter if you are fifteen years old or seventy-five. Taking action makes you a player. Inaction makes you a spectator. As a player, you will never again have to feel the pain of regret.

———

My father worked twelve-hour days in manual jobs his entire life. It was either noon to midnight or midnight to noon. As hard as he worked, his only asset was the house we lived in. I knew early on that I did not want to follow in my dad's footsteps.

But I did learn about work ethic. I also learned about taking action. I can remember being nine years old and working at my uncle's garbage collection business for five dollars a day. I can still remember the horrible garbage smell. I remember being embarrassed when friends would see me hanging off the side of the garbage truck. They were out having fun. I was working.

Yet even as a youngster, I recognized that I had to find a way to use this experience to my advantage. So I turned work into a game. The trash cans became weights and I would use them to become stronger. The clock became the opponent as I worked to see how fast we could go. The sooner we finished collecting the trash, the sooner we could go home. By hustling and working hard, I discovered that we could cut the collection time in half, turning an eight-hour day into a four-hour day. It was one of the first times I learned to turn something negative into something positive. And I used it to strengthen myself. That attitude would serve me well going forward.

As I grew older, I continued to take on several difficult jobs. I delivered drywall and loaded freight trucks. With each job, I found a way to turn it into a competition and tried to use it to better myself. Sometimes, we even made it fun. But all of these jobs taught me one thing; I did not want any of them to be a career choice.

As I entered my senior year of high school, I stared into an unknown future. Life's realities were waiting. I began to plan. Being a decent football player, I decided to write letters to Joe Paterno, the head football coach at Penn State University. I asked him to take a look at my football performance in the hopes of getting a scholarship. Even back then, I was aiming high. I wanted to play at the highest level.

After the football season, coach Paterno actually came to Norwin High School in Western Pennsylvania where I grew up. This was really exciting because few people of Paterno's stature ever came to our small town of Irwin. In fact, our home town newspaper published an article about his visit. I had been voted the MVP of our conference and I thought that Penn State might be my future.

But I was soon to be disappointed. He thanked me for the sincere letters but Penn State had already targeted other athletes at my position. No scholarship, no Penn State football.

However, that's not the end of the story. As it happened, the Ohio State Football staff read the article and thought I might be worth a look. The legendary head coach Woody Hayes also came to visit. Coach Hayes asked me, "Have you ever thought about going to Ohio State?"

I answered, "Coach, it's the only place I ever wanted to go."

My action had created an opportunity. The letters that I had sent coach Paterno set off a series of events that eventually put Woody Hayes in my living room. Had I not taken action, I might never have gone to Ohio State University; I might never have been seen by Chicago Bear scouts, and I might never have played in the NFL.

My life would have been completely different – and the pain of regret might have haunted me forever.

Ironically, I ran into Joe Paterno during my time with the Chicago Bears. I was filming a TV commercial in New York City with Pittsburgh Steelers running back Rocky Bleier. As we were walking into the studio to begin filming, coach Paterno was walking out. Joe immediately saw Rocky, who he was friends with, and they began a conversation. As they were talking, Rocky began to introduce me to Joe. But before Rocky could finish, Joe interrupted and said, "I know Doug Plank! I have not made many mistakes in my life, but he was one of them."

———

As the story above demonstrates, taking action and initiative in a proactive manner can lead to unknown opportunities.

Just like the 46 defense advocated, whenever possible, act first. Get off first. Take the initiative. Life is simpler when you have a plan and you are executing that plan. When you're doing that, you're not reacting. You're being proactive. When you're proactive, you're not sitting back letting the tidal wave of life's haphazard events roll over you. You're getting things done. You're creating opportunities. This has the added benefit of opening up a network of unknown possibilities.

On the other hand, thinking reactively has an inherent quality of fear. Reactive thinking requires that you begin to think about what you're going to do and how you're going to do it only after an event has begun. It is passive. It is defensive. It is more spectator-oriented than player-oriented. When you are trapped in reactive thinking, you will always be one step behind, scrambling to catch up. Catching up requires extra steps. It complicates everything.

The lesson? *Don't live a life of reaction!*

Nothing gets done without action. There have been many great ideas that were never acted upon. Without action, there can be no enthusiasm, motivation, or momentum. There have been many intelligent leaders that have failed to act on their words. Words matter when they have been delivered on a platform of emotion and aimed at each individual's heart.

Does enthusiasm come before action or does action come before enthusiasm? I contend that a call to action comes only after words are spoken. Words are the most important element in getting people to act.

Communication is the first step in achieving anything. There must be a plan in place for success to happen. Those that fail to plan, plan to fail. The basics of the 46 defense were preparation, anticipation, execution, and communication. The defense was based on the tendencies of the opponent. As such, we would design the defense based on the formation of the offense. We were ready with the best defense for whatever plays the offense ran from that formation. We took away their strengths and ignored decoys and motions they would use to confuse us.

This philosophy can also be applied to daily life. We need to be enthused and driven to succeed in our lives. We need to be aware of our opponent's intentions and goals. *Too many people chase decoys that have no impact on their lives. They decide to major in minor things.* This will effectively waste time that could be used towards great accomplishments.

We must remember that life is very much like a game. There is a start and a finish. We will be touching upon this concept throughout the book. In the game of life, many of us are closer to the finish than the start. We cannot waste our time and effort. We must focus on accomplishing our goals within a specific period of time.

———

The Chicago Bear 46 defense was all about aggressive attack. There was no waiting or reacting to what the offense did. *It was always attack – and that is fundamental to the "46 Attack Mindset."*

I have always lived aggressively. Living passively diminishes the quality of who you are and most importantly, who you're capable of being. When we sit back and wait, it's generally because we're constricted by some form of fear. This is like being trapped in a kind of living death. There is nothing worse than walking around in a live body with a dead spirit!

Living aggressively means not wasting the opportunity that is your life. Why waste the beauty, the magnificence and unbelievable energy that you have been given. Living in reaction is to always be one step behind. It means trying to counter moves that have already taken place. If you walk around reacting in fear, you miss your ability to choose and take action.

What is fear really? Fear is essentially the perception of an unknown threshold. It begins with an internal conversation about what you think is going to happen. How much pain and sacrifice will I have to endure? In reality, you don't know how much pain and sacrifice, if any, you will endure.

In fact, you don't know what's going to happen five years from now or even five minutes from now. It makes no sense to be afraid of what you don't know.

Two thousand years ago the great Roman Stoic philosopher Seneca said, "We suffer more in imagination than in reality."

What was true then remains true today.

Isn't it interesting that most fears are learned? Children are born fearless. We acquire fear through personal experience and what we absorb from other people. Fear is primarily a learned phenomenon.

To combat fear, stay centered on our question, "What do I need to get done?" To the degree that you're connected to the thing you need to get done, fear will diminish. When you are completely engrossed and focused in an activity, you are too mentally occupied to be afraid. You are focused on the next step. All of your attention is on moving forward.

Fear will not grow when you are completely dialed in to your present-moment task. There are many acronyms using the word "fear." The most common one is "False Evidence Appearing Real." Another one is "Face Everything and Rise."

The most important concept to remember about fear is that you need to recognize it and act on it with a plan of action.

———

I wish that just once in everyone's life, they had the opportunity to cover a kickoff. It is the very definition of being immersed in the present moment. It's a complete adrenaline rush. Running full speed and knowing that you are going to launch yourself into either a ball carrier, a blocker or maybe even three guys forming a blocking wedge (no longer legal) requires the very essence of the "46 Attack Mindset."

My job on kickoff returns was to occupy and take out the best tackler on my side of the field. That allowed other players to focus on blocking for the kick returner. Whether on offense or defense, every special teams play required 100% old school hustle and effort. There was never room for fear in this scenario. It required complete concentration on the job.

Most importantly, it was never about what they were going to do to me. It was always about w*hat I was going to do to them! This is how you move through fear!*

Kickoff coverage was the very essence of aggressive attack. I was so physically and emotionally amped and so focused on my task that nothing else mattered. It was complete absorption in the present moment. There was no thought of yesterday or tomorrow. It was right now and the only thought I had was running full speed at my target.

What if you approached every day as if you were on kickoff coverage? What if you aggressively attacked each day with the kind of energy and focus that a kickoff coverage requires?

I guarantee that you would be a real-life special teams all-star within weeks. *But it requires everything you have.* It requires the courage of 100% commitment, 100%

proactivity and 100% aggression. It all gets back to living each day as if it's your last.

You say you can't do that? Stay with me. You are about to learn how to bring everything you have every single day. In the world of football, I was able to suppress my survival instincts in order to play without fear or threat of injury. In real life, the "46 Attack Mindset" will allow you to overcome adversity and succeed despite setbacks. Adversity will teach you what "not to do" and you will become stronger and more focused on your goals. Ultimately, you will become...

Unstoppable.

Chapter Two – Bring Your "A" Game: 100% All the Time

The good players, the guys with talent, they have an A game, a B game, a C game. They don't feel perfect, it's practice, OK, go with the B game. I didn't have that option. There was only the A game for me—as hard as I could every time or I would not be on the field; that's what gave me such intensity.

Doug Plank

The quote above speaks to the idea that competition is real. You can choose not to compete, but the competition is going on whether or not you acknowledge it. If you are involved in sports, business or relationships, competition exists. If you choose to be complacent and not compete, unless you are immeasurably talented, you will be passed by and left behind. And the fault will be yours. Don't let that happen.

In this chapter, we will begin to understand the tools necessary to unleash our maximum intensity. We will explore just what constitutes your "A" game and why you need it to reach the upper limits of your genetic potential.

What does it mean to bring your "A" game? It typically means that an athlete or performer has committed to bringing their best effort and all of their skill to their craft. Certainly, 100% intensity and our best effort is difficult to bring all of the time. Most people have convinced themselves that it cannot be done.

But difficult is not the same as impossible – as we will see.

––––

Consider Thomas Edison and the electric light bulb. What about the Wright brothers and flight? How about going to the moon?

What do all of these have in common?

All of these accomplishments came to fruition because certain human beings chose to be unreasonable. Each of these achievements were once considered impossible. It took people with vision, belief, resolve and stamina to make the impossible possible.

We think we're not capable. We think that we could never achieve that kind of greatness. In fact, the same human universal intelligence that ran through the go-getters mentioned above runs through all of us. We've just never learned to tap into it.

I learned to reach the upper limits of my own potential almost out of necessity. Otherwise, I might have had to live the life of my father. I guarantee you that no one thought an undersized kid from a tiny town in Pennsylvania, who only started five games in college, would ever become an eight-year starter in the NFL – and actually have an impact on how the game is played.

That story is my version of going to the moon. I'm sure many people, and sometimes even me, figured I'd have a better shot at a lunar landing than leading the Chicago Bears in tackles as a rookie at a position I'd never played. No reasonable person would have given me a chance to do that.

So how did it happen?

I had to become unreasonable.

I had to step into the uncertainty of opportunity.

I said yes when they asked me if I'd ever played safety. In fact, I had never played safety.

But I knew that if they just gave me the chance, they would never regret it. I would give every fiber of my being to the opportunity.

To succeed, I had to generate almost superhuman energy and commit all of my attention to learning the position. I had to generate daily enthusiasm with my actions in order to create the emotions necessary to continue when any reasonable person would have quit. I had to harden myself and play through pain, injury and physical impairment that few NFL players today would even consider.

As my quote at the beginning of the chapter indicates, I could not afford the luxury of a B or a C game. There are no "participation trophies" in the NFL. It was imperative that I find a way to bring my "A" game in every possible moment. This sometimes made me difficult to deal with because more gifted people assumed I would just let up on the gas pedal in practices. After all, letting up was the norm for them. But in the reality of competition, which was every day for me, letting up on the gas pedal was not an option if I was going to stay employed.

So how is it possible to bring 100% intensity all of the time? Isn't that a truly unreasonable expectation?

The answer once again lies in the present moment. In reality, right now is the only place where life can be lived. The past is gone and the future has not yet happened. Here is why this is important:

Right now, in this moment, is when you make the choice to bring your "A" game. Right now is when you commit to bringing that 100% full throttle intensity. If you start thinking about the future and how tired you'll be or how tired you were ten minutes ago, you will convince yourself not to bring your best effort. That's called being reasonable.

But you're not living in the future, you're living right now. All of your power exists in the now. And you're learning how to become unreasonable.

If you make the commitment, you can bring everything you have to this moment. You can bring all of your mental and physical energy. And when the next moment arrives, you can bring everything in that moment as well. This is simply about bringing your *best self* to each moment.

I'm going to show you how – and if you make this a practice, pretty soon it becomes a habit. It's a habit that involves *controlling your mind*. Once you have learned mastery over your own mind and all the voices within, whole new worlds of possibility open up. You can overcome that quitting conversation that stops almost everyone else. You can suppress that survival instinct that keeps you from becoming your best self. And what you once thought was unreasonable and impossible, becomes your baseline level of effort.

——

Your mind is a mechanism. Its primary function is to help you survive. It does not care if you are interested in conquering a great goal. As such, it has the power to hinder you and hold you back. It simply wants to keep you safe.

Our mind generates thoughts – and although our thinking sometimes seems random, we have the ability to be in charge of the thoughts we put into our head. (If that's not true, send someone else off to therapy and you'll get better. It never works.)

The mind is completely at our disposal to use. *But we need to use it – before it uses us.*

Because the mind wants us to survive, it is characterized by a constant running dialogue that is always interpreting stimuli and evaluating options. Part of that dialogue is that the world is a dangerous place. And the mind will convince you that it is dangerous to bring 100% intensity all of the time. After all, that's unreasonable. It will remind you of all the perils and risks that exist. It will run all of the negative scenarios and pitfalls of going all out.

Your mind is simply trying to protect you. Again, it wants you to stay safe. It wants you to take the easy path. But once you recognize in real time when this internal dialogue has begun, you can take the first step towards understanding that you can shut down this *"Don't do it"* self-talk. In taking control of this inner dialogue, you can begin the process of suppressing your survival instincts.

Here is why this is important. If you think about it, *most of the time, your life is not actually in danger; your survival is not at stake.* Yes, you might be embarrassed. Yes, you might not get the result you were looking for. Yes, you might get frustrated or tired. But survival? It's generally not an issue.

This is important because when you look at great inventors, athletes, artists, or business people, you see people who are inherently aggressive. These are people who dare to do great things. They don't look at the day-to-day issues we all confront as matters of survival. They understand that difficult challenges or embarrassing outcomes are not life and death.

These aggressive achievers are not inherently better people than the rest of us. They simply face major challenges head-on and work hard to overcome them. They evaluate the obstacles and begin working smart in order to overcome them. Working smart is more important than working hard. Working smart will point you in the right direction and keep you from repeating the mistakes of the past.

People who adopt the "46 Attack Mindset" do not let the random musings of their mind stop them from attempting great things. They recognize when their minds are trying to get them to take the easy path and they redirect their thinking to what they want to get done!

This is the essence of bringing your "A" game. You must take control of your mind in the present moment and direct it to the task you need to accomplish.

If you study the people who do this, you'll also find that they do not ask for permission to begin their journey. They simply choose to take the first step. That step leads to the next step. Even though their minds warn them of failure, and their running dialogue tells them of all the bad things that could happen, they redirect that dialogue and begin a process of getting up and moving towards a target that they never let go of. Along this path, there are no guarantees of success. But by continuing to always aggressively move towards their target, they get closer and closer until they can't help but succeed. And they never quit visualizing it, and they never quit pursuing it.

These great achievers understand how to master the weapons of the mind.

⸺

We are now going to examine *all* of the weapons of the mind. These weapons are the tools you need to bring your "A" game.

Over time, bringing your "A" game becomes a habit. Overcoming adversity becomes a skill and an expectation. Most importantly, reaching the upper limits of your genetic potential becomes a reality.

Let's break down these tools.

Your "A" game consists of:

- Attitude
- Aggression
- Anticipation
- Adversity: Adapt and Overcome
- Accountability
- Accomplishment

Attitude

Ability tells us what you are capable of, but it is your attitude that determines how well you will accomplish the task. Everything begins with attitude. Life is about 10% of what happens to you and 90% of what you do about it. Without the proper attitude, you will never approach your potential.

My attitude has always been, when you're going to do something and you have a passion about it, why not be the best you can be?

Like your thoughts, your attitude is a choice. Your attitude will determine your mental fitness which is directly related to your outward behavior. It determines how you look, act, and what you say.

In any situation, you are either an asset or a liability. Being an asset begins with your attitude. It involves having the intention of adding value to whatever room you enter. It means focusing on solutions and not fixating on problems.

Being a liability means that you are contributing to the problem. You are sucking energy from your environment and adding no value. This helps no one, particularly yourself.

You've probably known people who are simply a drain to be around. They are often called energy vampires. These people are toxic and they rob you of your time and attention. It's been said that we are the average of the five people we spend the most time with. I remember a huge poster hanging on the wall of our Ohio State athletic facility. It was right above the main door as you exited the building. It said, "YAWYAW." It was simply an acronym for "You are who you associate with."

Truer words were never spoken. It's difficult to soar with the eagles if you are spending time with the turkeys. Be diligent in choosing your companions. Don't hang out with people who bring you down, or tell you what you can or can't do. Don't give your power away to people like that. Just as importantly, don't be one of those toxic people yourself.

When you associate with people who have positive attitudes, you can work together to share problems and find solutions. Adopt a philosophy of "Don't just find a fault, find a solution."

If you find yourself complaining, commit to finding *two* solutions.

Success is not an accident. Find people who have achieved what you want to achieve and study how they did it. Seek out knowledgeable and accomplished professionals and learn from them. Take on the attitude of a life-long learner. The eagles are out there but you have to reach out to them. If you can bring value to their world, even better. If you can be of service, they will be even more apt to share knowledge and wisdom with you.

———

To be successful, you need a baseline level of skill in whatever you're doing in order to take full advantage of the "46 Attack Mindset." Your skill then gives you even greater confidence as you continue to grow in your competence and ability.

To gain this competence, you must take charge of your own development. You must determine the talents, skills and abilities that can take you to the next level – and the next. Then you must make whatever investment is necessary in time and money to get those skills.

In addition to traditional classroom education, the three quickest paths to competence are 1) learning by doing, 2) reading and 3) listening to recorded material. It's a sad commentary on our society that only one in twenty Americans reads something daily. Consider this carefully: a person that does not read is no better than a person that *cannot* read.

Books provide us with reference experiences of people who have accomplished things beyond us. They offer us models of possibility for what we might achieve – and often give us the methods and means to go about it. Life-long learners always allow some time to read and better themselves each day.

Mike Ditka, the all-time great Chicago Bear player and later my coach once said, "A smart man learns from his own mistakes, a wise man learns from others' mistakes – and a dumb donkey will keep doing the same thing over and over."

Having the attitude of a life-long learner postures us to be an asset and to continue working towards the possibility of making the last thing we ever do, the greatest thing we ever do. And that's another unreasonable idea worth striving for.

———

In the lexicon of high performers, there is a saying. "See it, believe it, and achieve it."

This maxim has existed since the days of the iconic author Earl Nightingale for a reason. It works. If it didn't, it would have disappeared from the American vocabulary long ago.

These seven simple words comprise an attitude that captures vision, planning, and execution in an easy-to-remember form. These words have been repackaged and reiterated in any number of ways but we're going to keep it uncomplicated.

Here's a straightforward example of "see it, believe it, and achieve it" in a real setting. When I began writing letters to coach Paterno, my vision was to play division one college football at Penn State. In my mind I "saw" myself playing division one and winning in that scenario.

I genuinely "believed" that I would achieve this goal and I continually saw it happening in my mind. I acted as if it was going to come true and all of my behaviors supported that belief.

Even though I did not end up at Penn State, I "achieved" my goal of playing division one football. The fact that it was at Ohio State actually worked to my advantage in the long run.

Seeing and believing are a form of expectation. When you expect something to happen, you tend to look for it and your behavior supports that expectation. There are several studies that have demonstrated that grade school teachers who have been told they are teaching high potential students treat those students differently. Even when those students were average or below, they overachieved because their teachers expected more of them.

Like those teachers who believed in their students, our expectations tend to create reality. We need to pay attention to what we believe is true because we will often find it. If we expect to find rude and angry people, we are apt to find them. If, on the other hand, we expect to find polite and happy people, they are more likely to show up. Our attention goes to what we are looking for.

This is why it's important to have clear expectations of what we believe is true. We will discover that whatever we focus on usually comes true. By passionately pursuing our expectations, we will attract people and ideas that will move us closer to our goals.

Seeing and believing are integral parts of any successful attitude and it means having a plan. I had a game plan every time I stepped onto the football field at both the college and professional levels. Some people might have thought that I took it to extremes but planning gave me a significant competitive advantage.

Even though I was strong and aggressive, I was often up against bigger and faster opponents. So I planned to learn everything I could about them. I looked at film to study their tendencies, their strengths, weaknesses, habits and histories. I learned about every possible aspect of their game.

I then imagined every possible game scenario in my mind. Over and over I saw myself perfectly executing tackles, blitzes and pass coverages. The night before the game, I would dream about playing that game in my mind. I would see the people I was playing against and while this didn't guarantee success, more often than not, things played out in reality just as they had in my mind. By the time I stepped onto the field, it was as if I was on a roller coaster going straight ahead. I didn't even have to think. I was programmed for success; locked and loaded.

I recall watching film of the great Houston running back, Earl Campbell, with our defensive unit before a game with the Oilers. Earl had thighs bigger than most people's waists, 34 inches. He made a career of running over people. On one play, we watched Earl break through the line. Denver Bronco safety Steve Foley came up to make the tackle.

The next thing we saw was Foley putting his helmet into one of Earl's mammoth thighs. It did not end well. We watched as poor Steve Foley got carried out on a stretcher, knocked out cold.

Our defensive coach, Buddy Ryan, always made of point of challenging us during our week of preparation. Buddy turned off the film and said, "If any of you guys don't want to play this weekend, just let me know." Essentially, Buddy challenged our manhood.

I immediately thought to myself, *Earl Campbell is not running over Doug Plank this weekend.*

That week, I continually visualized Earl breaking through the line and me making what we used to call, a "business decision."

This business decision centered on what we talked about earlier in the player versus spectator question. It wasn't about what Earl was going to do to me. *It was all about what I was going to do to him.* I took great pride in my reputation as a hitter and I vowed that I would change Earl's game before he changed mine.

Well, I don't know exactly how much I changed Earl's game but having visualized planting my helmet between Earl's thighs for an entire week prepared me for the reality when it happened. The results are on YouTube. Planting my helmet at full speed into his most vulnerable area, I knocked Earl out of the game. But being the great back that he was, he returned to the game with even greater purpose and determination.

Earl was a terrific player and I have nothing but respect for him. But I was faced with these business decisions weekly and had I not proactively visualized and carried them out, my tenure in the NFL would have been short-lived.

I truly believe that the more you think about your goals, the more you activate the law of attraction. Whether in sports, business, or relationships, the more you visualize what you want, the more you will attract the people, ideas, opportunities, and resources that will bring you closer to them. It all comes back to what you expect.

———

There is yet another aspect of the "see it, believe it, and achieve it" maxim that is worth exploring. When you expect to succeed, your field of vision expands to see opportunities that others miss. The very act of believing and expecting also convinces others that you know what you're doing. It can change how reality unfolds.

Consider that so much of life involves acting. When you act as if you are a success, you often generate the feelings and characteristics of more talented and qualified people. The old adage, "Fake it 'til you make it" has a lot of truth in it. If you continue to fake it, while developing skills and competencies along the way, you begin to *believe* you're that successful person. Eventually, you actually *become* the person you once pretended to be.

It's all about the power of belief. Isn't it interesting that in the NFL, scoring increases 300% in the last two minutes of each half? Why is that?

It's because the offense "believes" they are going to score. There is an urgency and focus that the clock imposes that brings belief to the forefront. Then, after the offense creates a successful play or two, the defense also begins to believe that they will be scored upon. They start playing on their heels and lose their aggressive mindset. It's the same in business.

After football, I owned several Burger King franchises. I had a partner in that venture who came at everything with a strong message. He was driven to succeed like no one I had ever seen. In fact, he was the Bobby Knight of Burger King. He would throw chairs and yell at the top of his lungs. I actually saw him make grown men cry. I swear, the man had catsup running through his veins! He expected to succeed – and he did.

But not only was he aggressive and consumed with belief, he was also incredibly organized and motivated. He helped others see and believe by making difficult and complex operations simple. He created a program called "Follow the Dots." In this program, every job description in the restaurant was posted in great detail. This eliminated any doubt about what you were supposed to do. He had a vision with a plan, he believed it would work, and he implemented it.

In implementing the "see it, believe it, and achieve it" mantra, he told employees how to do it; he showed them how to do it; and then he empowered them to go do it. If you can implement a simple "no fail" system like this into your plan, your chances of success will improve ten-fold.

————

Also, within the "A" game category of attitude, it's worth mentioning the notion of personal pride. We have a crisis in our country. Only about 20% of Americans are in satisfactory physical shape. Almost 80% of us are overweight – and many are clinically obese.

There are many factors that have contributed to this. Sugar, processed food and alcohol are abundantly available. Jobs that once required physical labor are no longer the norm. But ultimately, we need to have the attitude that, at least for ourselves, being unhealthy is no longer acceptable. We have to take the responsibility for educating ourselves and making better nutritional and exercise choices.

The "46 Attack Mindset" will help in this process. The mind leads the body. Taking control of your mind and attitude, as you are learning in this section, is fundamental to making better choices and taking action. Make it a habit to make present moment choices that serve you. Right now, don't eat that cake. Later on, you can revisit whether or not you want it. When later becomes "right now," once again simply stay present and don't eat the cake. These present moment choices create the momentum that will lead you to victory.

Take an active role in your own health. See it, believe it, and achieve it. Implement the knowledge that already exists – and in time, you will be the person you have visualized.

Aggression

The second component of our "A" game is aggression. The word aggression has gotten a bad rap because it's often used in the context of war. In fact, the Latin root of the word aggressive is "to move toward." I suggest that we move more aggressively towards life-affirming activities and always go after the experience of living.

The antonym or opposite of the word aggression is "defense." Somewhat ironically, the famous 46 Bear defense is probably the most aggressive football defense ever conceived. It aggressively attacked the supposed aggressor (the offense) to the point where the offense often became completely defensive.

While that may sound confusing, it's actually quite simple. It goes back to the idea of being proactive and getting off first. The 46 defense attacked. The offense then reacted. If you are the first to initiate, you are the aggressor.

I encourage you to use the concept of aggression in the most positive ways. For example, be the first to help someone. Be the first to attempt something others are too scared to try.

Make the sales call you've been putting off. Make the phone call to the person you always wanted to meet. Introduce yourself to someone you've been too afraid to approach. Call someone simply to tell them how much you appreciate them and the difference they've made in your life.

Aggressively make someone's day! Leave every environment you enter better than how you found it. Chances are, great things will happen. If great things don't happen, so what. *You're stronger and better for having made the attempt.*

Remember, the pain of execution is temporary. The pain of regret is forever. Don't wait.

———

For a moment, let's examine the connection between aggression and anger. Angry is generally not the best way to go through life. But there are times and places when it can be very useful. Once again, it requires using your mind in the most productive way.

One of the quotes I'm most known for is, *"Most football players are temperamental. That's 90 percent temper and 10 percent mental."*

Why does the word "temperamental" resonate with football players? Most people think of football players as angry, mad, stupid human beings. Just look at a team photo of any college football team. That team picture will never be confused with the graduating class of the medical school. The majority of players are staring straight ahead with the look of anger. The second thing you notice is the number of people that look like they weigh 300 pounds. This is a group of hungry, angry men with tempers and yet they must maintain a minimum of mental acuity to continue to play.

Our head coach at Ohio State was the legendary Woody Hayes. Woody was a very emotional, energetic, and patriotic man. He had coached football at Ohio State for a long time. He wanted his teams to play with passion, anger, and intensity. He always said "I have never seen a player make a tackle with a smile on his face." It was safe to say that the majority of his players were indeed temperamental, intense, focused, and intent on executing their assignments.

The majority of the Ohio State players were on an athletic scholarship. Most of them spent their time in football meetings, lifting weights, hitting dummies or each other. They had to maintain a C average in all classes to participate in football. The school would hire tutors that would spend hours tutoring the slower learning players to attain sufficient grade point averages. In some years, this required many tutors. The plays called on the field were simple. The defensive plays to the right of the center used even numbers and the plays to left of the center used odd numbers. The backfield players were given numbers 1,2,3, or 4. Still, as simple as it was, the players made many mistakes.

What word describes an action to perform a simple assignment while under the emotional and physical duress of getting hit, while filled with anger, suffering pain, suffering more pain, and while deciding what your next move will be? That word is temperamental. That is 90% temper and 10% mental. That is the bones of a football player.

When I played football, I played angry. It might sound childish, but I would trick my mind into believing that the person on the other side had done something to me or my family and now it was time to deliver justice. I would think nasty thoughts about the players I'd be going against. It sounds shallow, but I had to work myself into a fury. I had bad intentions from the moment I took the field. By controlling my mind and my internal conversation, I could direct my behavior towards what had to be done. That's what worked for me. Something else might work for you.

A cadre of mental toughness coaches and sports psychologists often refer to this "angry approach" as accessing your dark side. In this instance, the dark side is simply the ability to put aside the cultural programming that tells you to be nice, be gentle, and never hurt anyone else. The dark side allows you to inflict justifiable harm and pain when the situation is appropriate.

If you think this is somehow wrong, consider how you would behave if someone was trying to harm your spouse, child or loved one. Hopefully, you would access this dark side rather quickly and do whatever needed to be done to eliminate the threat. If you did, you would be completely justified.

Football is a violent game and it is meant to be played all out. When I played, no one on either side of the line of scrimmage showed any mercy. I was no exception. I recall that at least one team had a bounty on me due to my reputation as a hard hitter. That meant that if someone could knock me out of the game, that person would get extra cash.

Bounties were not common during my time in the NFL. Big hits and big plays would be rewarded if the Bears won the game. It was never connected to a particular player or a particular team. It was usually a free dinner at a nice restaurant downtown. These rewards vanished when they became known to the general public and the NFL.

Once, playing against the Denver Broncos, I recall hearing that a bounty had been put out on me. As I went to make a tackle on the sidelines, I let up for just a moment. I got completely leveled by the ball carrier. He got up talking smack and muttering something about me not being so tough.

Well, I'm telling you, it was as if his words had shot some kind of superhero adrenaline through my veins. I got up and vowed that on the next play, someone was going to pay. Now, please understand, I'm not necessarily proud of this, but again, it was a tough business.

On the very next play, it was as if I had been shot out of a cannon. I launched myself into an unsuspecting pulling guard with all of the force and torque I could muster. I effectively ended his season.

Here's the point of this story. *The difference on that particular play was how I used my mind.* I was the very same person that had been leveled on the play before. But with focused mental intensity, I reached the upper limits of my genetic potential because I was mentally prepared and bringing everything I had in that moment. I made a decision. I *chose* to be the ultimate aggressive warrior in that moment. In that instance, I used anger and pride to motivate me.

26

I encourage you to find whatever it is that will motivate you as well. Whatever it is, choose it in the moment that you need to produce and perform. That's what the "46 Attack Mindset" is all about. *When you choose to bring all of your mental and physical attention to the task at hand, you will bring results unlike you have ever previously produced.* Once you've practiced bringing yourself present to the moment, you'll find it getting easier. And remember, it's never about what's going to happen to you. It's always about what you're going to get done – and in the example above – what I was going to do to them.

As part of this mindset, I challenge you to be a cause and not the effect of something caused. When I got leveled by the ball carrier in the example above, something "happened" to me. I was the recipient of another person's aggression. On the next play, I chose to be the cause.

In every moment of every game, I wanted to be a cause and not an effect. I trained my mind to instruct my body to hit as hard as I possibly could. That was my job. I wanted to know that when I left the field, there was not one more thing I could have done. I wanted our opponents and the players I played against to remember that they had played against Doug Plank.

———

Let's consider another context in which aggressive anger can be useful and appropriate. Humans are the only life form that get to choose to do less than their best. Think about it. Trees grow as high as they can. Squirrels store up as many nuts as they can. Bees make as much honey as possible.

Unlike them, we humans almost always choose to do less than we can. Once again, this is our mind telling us that we need to conserve our energy. But these "do less than we can" choices train us to be emotionally weak. Eventually, this weakness becomes a habit.

Whenever our mind is faced with the choice of going all out, it convinces us that it's dangerous and a threat. It convinces us that making a change will be terribly uncomfortable and that we should resist what would actually be in our own best interests. This emotional weakness keeps us from pursuing important goals and even encourages mediocrity. Once again, it's our survival instinct trying to keep us comfortable.

So what should we do?

Get angry!

If you're overweight, get angry!

If you're broke, get angry!

If you're scared, get angry!

Draw a line in the sand and say, *"Enough!"*

You no longer need to live like this. You no longer need to accept mediocrity. You no longer need to squander the amazing life and the opportunities that you have been given. Indifference and denial are diseases and you can attack them!

Right now, in this moment, get angry and own your circumstances. This is on you. This doesn't make you a bad person. It makes you a reasonable human being. But we are no longer going to be reasonable. *We're all about being unreasonable*!

If up until this point in your life you have made undisciplined or weak choices, that's fine. But no more! No more excuses. Ben Franklin said that he who is good at making excuses, is seldom good at anything else.

The excuses end now!

Simply state what you will no longer tolerate. I'm here to help you. Write down what you're going to do; create your plan. Then lock and load and begin right now to take the necessary actions. Every day.

Being unreasonable is rarely comfortable. But neither is the greatness that comes with reaching the upper limits of who you can be. Use appropriate anger as a tool to get you to where you want to go. Elevate your baseline level of effort.

The new you; the best you – is right within your grasp.

———

Anticipation

The third component of our "A" game is anticipation. Anticipation really gets back to planning and the "see it" part of see it, believe it and achieve it. To truly win in life, you must have a plan. But before you can create a viable plan, you need to have a vision.

Vision must precede everything else. As you examine your life, you must know where you are and where you want to go. This requires vision.

It's amazing just how many people work hard every day yet are not particularly productive. This is simply because they are not working with any goals or objectives in mind. They spin their wheels on the treadmill of life but end up nowhere. They are simply busy. They have no vision.

People who reach the upper limits of their potential never mistake activity for accomplishment. Your ultimate goal must come from a clearly defined vision. This vision must be realistically attainable based on a logical, well-conceived plan.

Perhaps the best example of this in my life came when Mike Ditka became head coach of the Chicago Bears in 1982. His vision and mission for our team was clear: win the Super Bowl. Before Ditka arrived, the only mention of the Super Bowl in Chicago was that every NFL player received two complimentary tickets.

Ditka created a detailed plan that clearly outlined the expectations and sacrifices necessary to reach the Super Bowl. He also emphasized that this would require a change of personnel such that many of the players he was addressing at the time would no longer be there. He explained that you need the right people in the right positions before any strategic planning could properly be executed.

A few years later, I took this lesson to heart when I owned several Burger King restaurants. Personnel decisions were incredibly important. I had to ensure that people were in jobs that were the right fit for their skillset. Some people were better with customers. Some were better in food preparation. Ditka was right. It was essential to the smooth operation of the business that people were in the right positions and set up to succeed.

Planning is important for a variety of reasons. We often hear about "climbing the ladder of success." When creating your plan, it's essential that you carefully select the exact goal you want to achieve. Otherwise, you might find that you've "climbed the ladder" only to find that you placed the ladder on the wrong wall.

A proper plan begins with the end in mind. Ditka began with the understanding that winning the Super Bowl was the desired result. Like him, you must also know exactly what goal you are trying to achieve. You can then work backwards from your desired end result to plot the steps you need to attain your goal.

———

Within the category of Anticipation, it's important to address preparation as part of the planning process. One minute of preparation is worth ten minutes of execution. The secret of success is your daily schedule.

Football taught me to have a script for every day. A script keeps you ahead of the competition. Living life as a player and not as a spectator requires a plan for every day. With a script that you've written out and visualized, your chances of success multiply and your accomplishments will more than likely inspire others.

Having a plan for every day also simplifies things. You don't have to think about your next step if it's already scripted. I believe in the Kiss and Kill principles: KISS stands for "Keep it Simple Stupid." KILL stands for "Keep it Learnable and Likeable."

When possible, "KISS and KILL" complexity in your plan. Executing on a simple plan saves time and energy. Drive complexity out of your life whenever possible.

———

No matter who you work for or what your title is, it's useful to think of yourself as a corporation of one. Each of us is essentially our own personal services corporation. We are the architect of our own destiny and we get to write the script. We are all free agents in life. That's part of the beauty of living in the United States of America. In the year 2020, there are no excuses left. There are many opportunities to get education, training and become exactly who you want to become. The question becomes, "Who do you want to be?"

Once you can answer that question, you *must* create a daily plan to get you there. You must schedule your fitness, your business, your studies, your family time and whatever is important to you. If it's on your daily schedule, it won't require motivation and willpower. You simply handle the allotted activity in the time you've allowed. You don't have to *feel* like doing it, you simply need to do it. If an important activity is in your daily plan, ultimately it becomes a habit.

Eventually you will be that "soaring eagle" that others want to emulate. You will inspire others by the example you set. Your daily routine will not only be a road map for your own success, it will also serve as a road map of success for others.

Whether scoring in the last two minutes of a half, or succeeding in a demanding business venture, once you have a proper plan, whatever you truly believe will happen will occur. If you have a burning desire to succeed, you will find the knowledge, finances, and talent to realize your vision.

The exercise in Appendix A is designed to help you to create your vision and plan. Remember, if you fail to plan, you can plan to fail.

———

Anticipation means looking at everything that could possibly happen. This implies two things. You must first control whatever is in your power to control. Have you done your homework? Have you studied everything about what you need to know? Are you in the best physical and mental condition that you can possibly be in, given your circumstances?

Second, you must look at contingencies. You need to anticipate what might happen if things go wrong. And yes, sometimes things go wrong no matter how well you've planned. That leads us into the next component of our "A" game.

Adversity: Adapt and Overcome

Stuff happens.

People break commitments.

Equipment breaks down.

Plans get derailed.

Injury, illness, divorce, bankruptcy … you name it.

The ability to overcome adversity is the number one key to success. This is critical to understand. You have to anticipate adversity in your life because it's going to show up. The people who look for the opportunity in adversity are the people who move ahead in life.

I'm not suggesting that you need to love adversity. But it's useful to recognize that most of your personal growth occurs under adverse circumstances. The strongest timber is a result of sustaining daily resistance from a strong wind. As I mentioned in our section on attitude, it's 10% what happens to you and 90% what you do with it. And while you don't need to love adversity, too many people run from challenge simply to avoid negative consequences.

Several years ago, I read an outstanding book by Paul Stolz called <u>The Adversity Quotient</u>. In it, he outlined three types of people. He called them quitters, campers and climbers. These three groups exist in both sports and life. They are not distinguished by characteristics like color, size, gender, or religion. They are distinguished by an internal state of mind.

Quitters rarely take on a challenge but when they do, they almost always quit at the first sign of failure. Many of them experience what's called learned helplessness. They don't believe that anything they do will have an impact on the outcome of their situation. This helplessness becomes a mental habit. Their internal conversation tells them that it is futile to try to change their situation because nothing they do will work. They give up. They make excuses for their inaction and often blame everyone but themselves for their sad circumstances.

At Ohio State, Woody Hayes referred to players who gave up as AYO's...All You Others. They were not bad athletes or players. But when these guys realized that they were not going to play, they quit trying at their peak level. They lacked both the patience and the resolve to improve their game.

Most people fall under the category of what Stolz called campers. Campers camp. They get halfway up the mountain of success and decide that they don't really want to go further. They make the decision to stop the pain and effort that it takes to get to the top. This actually describes most of America.

Campers become complacent, satisfied with their circumstances and they lose their ambition. They lack the proactive and aggressive mindset that characterizes the next group; the climbers.

Climbers climb. They never quit and they never camp. They are driven to make it to the top.

It's useful to note that just because someone is driven doesn't mean that they are dissatisfied with their life. Usually, it's the contrary. Climbers simply love the growth that comes from challenge. They love the fact that they continue to improve and bring more to the table. They have an unquenchable thirst to get better.

Climbers graduate but they never stop learning. They have that "life-long learning" attitude that we described as essential to our "A" game. They bring 100% effort all of the time. They recognize that the present moment is where life is lived and that is exactly when 100% is required.

Climbers move through obstacles to become the great innovators, CEOs, top salespeople and highest achieving professional athletes. These people never give up. Thomas Edison was the perfect example of the climber. When attempt after attempt at inventing the electric light bulb failed, he famously said, "I have not failed. I've just found 10,000 ways that won't work."

Thomas Edison had a mental approach that required experimentation until he got the result he wanted. Each try was a learning experience. Quitting was not an option. Imagine what you could achieve if you approached your goal as a series of experiments that only ended when you got what you were after.

Thomas Edison and his fellow climbers have always recognized that quitting is a choice. It's useful to understand just what quitting is. Quitting begins with an internal conversation that sounds something like this:

This is bull. I shouldn't have to do this. It's not fair. This is going to take too long. It's going to hurt. And finally…

I'm not going to do it.

The quitting conversation is a very reasonable one. Why? Because anything worth going after is going to be difficult. And it's probably going to be very uncomfortable. As such, it's perfectly logical to quit. I'll also bet that you can find one hundred people who would agree and say, "Of course you should quit. Who wouldn't?"

Climbers wouldn't, that's who.

Climbers recognize when this quitting conversation shows up and they immediately shut it down. They then shift their focus and internal conversation to what needs to get done.

Consider this. Not quitting is a trait that is available to everyone. It requires no skill. It requires no talent. Just like hard work, anyone can access this trait. It is an essential component of the "46 Attack Mindset" and like all of the components, it simply comes back to controlling your mind.

Those that do not quit understand that failure is often just part of the package. Quitting is a very reasonable thing to do. But the climbers, the go-getters, and those who adopt the "46 Attack Mindset" recognize that accomplishing something great requires you to be unreasonable. Like Thomas Edison, it requires the ability to look at failure after failure as part of a learning curve that eventually gets you to your goal.

Didn't work? So what. What did you learn? Like Edison, now you know what not to do. Keep trying.

Back in 2009, the financial world was in collapse. Like a number of people, I lost many of my assets during this downturn. I went through all three stages. I was initially a quitter, then a camper, and finally a climber. The good news is that you can change at any time. You can choose to be a climber. Once you do, you will become better and more determined.

Be a climber.

———

By now, you understand that adversity always shows up. Failure is part of the deal. But how you fail can help you deal with the inevitable adversity.

Like a ball carrier with a forward lean, you can still make progress when you're tackled. Even when you fall flat on your face, you can still fall forward for extra yardage.

Sometimes adversity shows up just to test how badly you want something. You must be prepared to handle any situation. I'm living proof that there is nothing you cannot accomplish if you keep trying.

Shortly after my football career was over, I went into Columbus, Ohio to open a Burger King restaurant. I did not realize it but my proposed restaurant was one mile away from another store owned by the largest franchisee in Columbus. He was using his influence to stop the construction of my restaurant in order to keep out competition. The vice president of the Midwest region told me to accept that the store would not be built and my franchisee status with Burger King was subject to cancellation.

As a climber, I was not going to give up. Recognizing that action always trumps inaction, I called the CEO of Burger King Corporation in Miami for five days in a row. Finally, on the fifth day, he returned my call. He apologized for the situation and said the vice president of the Midwest region would call me back within the next ten minutes. The VP grudgingly called me back and said the next restaurant built in Columbus was going to be mine.

A few years later, when I moved to Phoenix Arizona, I bought the franchise rights for a Mexican restaurant concept called Taco Cabana. I found out the hard way that Phoenix did not need another Mexican restaurant. I owned the business for 18 months and just could not make money. I sold the Taco Cabana equipment at a big loss.

But I learned from the experience. I was sure there were other people who had also had restaurants fail after opening. I began researching recently-closed Burger Kings and contacted the banks that financed their equipment. After a few days, the banks started to call. If the Burger King restaurant had been open less than one year, I would negotiate buying the equipment at 10% of the original cost and resell it for big profits to Burger King franchisees. I did exactly that and recovered my losses within a year.

The lesson? It's not how you start; it's how you finish.

———

Perhaps my first taste of soul-crushing adversity occurred my freshman year at Ohio State. It certainly taught me that adversity was going to be something I would need to anticipate going forward.

The Ohio State football team had just won a national championship the year before I arrived. At our first practice, I could not believe how huge and tough some of the players looked. They were grown men with wives and children. Many already had IRA'S, 401K's and 529 Education Savings accounts for their children!

What had I gotten myself into?

That first day proved to be a disaster. We practiced on a hard synthetic turf. We were not wearing pads; only helmets. The drills we were performing were meant to be walk-throughs. That meant they were done at slow speed and designed to be teaching tools.

But the slow speed was short-lived. As can happen when you have that many young men in one place, testosterone took over. Before long, everyone was tackling and hitting each other at full speed. I was running with the ball and tried to change direction. I was hit hard by another player from my blind side. I experienced a burning sensation in my right knee as I fell to the ground. The pain was incredible.

But the humiliating words of an assistant coach stung even more.

As I was lying on the ground grimacing in pain, the coach said, "Do you think the people in Irwin, Pennsylvania would be proud of you lying on the ground your first day at Ohio State?"

Words are powerful. Words can destroy a young man's confidence. It was a cruel comment but it sent me on a different path. I realized at that moment that I would have to change my conditioning and level of intensity or my entire football career might be in jeopardy.

In sports, injuries are often seen as a sign of weakness. Injuries indicate a lack of conditioning and proper training. The trainer diagnosed my condition as tendonitis. Tendonitis is a minor strain in the joints. He told me to put ice on it and let the orthopedic doctor look at it the following week.

Each day I came into the athletic facility and put ice on the knee hoping I could return in a couple of days. Despite using crutches, the knee continued to have major swelling the entire week. After seven days of ice and continued swelling, I went to the orthopedic surgeon.

He looked at my knee and asked me when this happened. He pulled and pushed on the knee and moved it from side to side.

After a few moments, he stopped and stared straight into my eyes. He said, "Doug, what is your phone number?"

For a moment, I thought he was going to call my parents to come and take me home. I slowly repeated my phone number.

He said, "Doug, I am scheduling surgery tomorrow morning and I need your parents to give me permission to operate. You have partially torn two ligaments, the ACL and MCL, and torn cartilage."

I was devastated.

That was my introduction to big-time college football. But from that experience, I learned the value of having a strength and conditioning program. I studied and learned everything I could about getting stronger. I took it upon myself to become as strong and as fast as I possibly could. This became one of my first experiences at overcoming serious adversity and working towards the upper limits of my genetic potential.

It also reinforced a question that I had been asking ever since I was working on the garbage truck at nine years of age. How can I use this to my advantage?

If you can find an answer to that question, and I guarantee that you can – you can begin to turn adversity around.

When was the last time that you had your world flipped upside down? How long did it take you to recover? Did you anticipate it and were you ready for it?

In college and pro sports, injuries are a way of life. They happen every day. Ninety percent of the players don't care about your problems and the other ten percent are simply glad it happened to you and not them. This is merely an aspect of competitive sports. You are no good to the team if you can't perform.

Sports is a microcosm of the larger society. Generally speaking, outside of family and close friends, no one cares much about your problems. In business, you are no good to your company if you can't perform. Certainly, your friends and work colleagues care about you. But they're going to continue with their work, with or without you.

It's important to condition yourself both mentally and physically for adversity to strike. Why? Because you are responsible for getting out of whatever turmoil you're in.

Whether it's because of injury or illness, or even losing your job, the sooner you can get back into the game, the better. You are only as good as your last performance. This is why, under stress, pressure, and adverse circumstances, the "46 Attack Mindset" is so necessary to adopt. This mindset brings you immediately into the present moment where you can take the appropriate action.

Let's face it. Life is often unfair. It's important to recognize that fairness is not a concept rooted in reality. Spiders eat flies. Birds eat worms. Big fish eat little fish. It's not fair to the flies, worms and smaller fish. But nature doesn't care. Fair or unfair, it's on you to recognize whatever adversity surrounds you and to deal with it appropriately.

I saw this all the time in the NFL. It was just business. If you were a great player but injured and no longer capable of performing, you were cut. Nothing personal, just business. Best of luck going forward.

I recall some of the game's greatest players towards the end of their careers. Guys like Joe Namath and O.J. Simpson; opponents wanted to get one last crack at them. In Joe Namath's last game, he was playing for the Los Angeles Rams. We upset the Rams on that day and I had two interceptions. It was a rough day for Joe but no one on our sidelines was feeling sorry for him. No one was rolling out the "victory tour red carpets" for star players as their careers came to a close. Players who were making a fraction of their salaries were practically licking their chops to get a good hit on them. It was like life in the jungle; only the strongest and swiftest survived.

I share these stories simply because adversity is undefeated. No matter who you are, it's going to arrive. So instead of withdrawing or freezing with indecision when times get tough, your new mindset will propel you into productive action – sooner rather than later. You will have already hardened yourself. This will differentiate you from most of your peers.

So I ask you, what adversity is holding you back? Are you refusing to deal with it? Take the action you need to take right now and continue to deal with your problems every day.

Remember, it's not about being knocked down. That's going to happen.

It's all about how soon you get up and get back into action.

Accountability

The fifth component of our "A" game speaks to accountability. You owe it to your family, your employer, your teammates and most of all, yourself, to hold yourself to the highest standard.

Earlier, I said that this book will be a chance for you to explore what price you are willing to pay to become your best. It is time for that exploration.

Truly reaching the upper limits of your genetic potential requires that you accept responsibility for everything that happens under your sphere of influence. This amounts to taking *unreasonable ownership* for your circumstances. Certainly, you cannot control what other people do. But you *can* influence them and you are in complete control of your own behavior. If you really examine your life, you will find that you are in far more control of what happens than you realize.

Consider that you are in control of and accountable for the following. I call these the 13 Elements of Control.

1. How you show up each day
2. How you look
3. What you say
4. How you listen to others
5. What you eat and drink
6. How often and how intelligently you exercise
7. Your education and what you read
8. The people who surround you
9. The news you consume
10. How you treat people and the success of your personal relationships
11. How you spend your time
12. Where you spend your time
13. Your income

Yes, even your income. Your income is determined by three factors: 1) What you do, 2) How well you do it and 3) The difficulty of replacing you.

If you make yourself impossible to replace, it won't matter how old you are, what gender, race or religion. If they can't live without you, you will have maximum income leverage.

To make yourself indispensable, become an expert at your business. Know your business inside and out. Be the best at what you do. Most business skills are learnable. Yes, this may require some time and patience. It will require making some mistakes and learning from experience. But the entire point of this book is that life, sports and business are difficult and hard. *To prevail, you must be harder!*

That's why the "46 Attack Mindset" exists. It exists to give you the competitive advantage that only an evolved and advanced mindset can provide.

Let's take a moment to examine these 13 Elements of Control in more detail.

1) *How you show up each day*: This primarily refers to your attitude and your energy. We addressed attitude separately as one of the components of your "A" game. Energy is something else. You must be intentional about bringing your best energy to each moment; particularly the moments where you need to influence an outcome.

I learned a lot of life lessons from Coach Woody Hayes at Ohio State, but perhaps the most important one was about energy. Woody taught us to bring energy and enthusiasm every single day. He taught us that we were responsible for bringing our own fire and inspiration to everything we did. He certainly injected those qualities into us, but under his influence, we learned how to bring them ourselves.

If you played football at Ohio State, you never just went through the motions. As I learned at my first day of practice when I was so badly injured, there really was no such thing as a "walk-through." Woody told us that you play the way you practice. And every practice had a purpose.

Because there was such great talent on the team and because Woody wasn't going to allow anything but our best effort, our practices were frequently brutal. In fact, games on Saturday were often a walk in the park by comparison.

Every practice was a lesson in how to prepare and how to win. I learned to play and practice at the highest tempo of which I was capable. Everything I did became "game tempo" and I tried to be clear that I was not just running around to play "paddy cake." It was 100% full throttle or nothing.

In order to compete, I needed to bring my "A" game every day and those early experiences at Ohio State informed me that excellence was no accident. I was surrounded by the best and I was determined to become one of them. This meant that I needed to show up with enthusiastic energy, concentrated attention, and the desire to run through a wall if that's what it took to be a national champion.

Ask yourself each day, "Am I showing up with my best?"

2) *How you look*: Humans are visual creatures. Right or wrong, you will be judged by how you present yourself. The good news is – you get to choose how you present yourself to the world. The bad news is – you don't get to choose how other people perceive you. I would only suggest that you bring your best authentic self to the world, whatever that looks like, and be aware that everyone's tastes differ.

It only makes sense that if you want to work in corporate America, you make some effort to fit in visually. If you want to be a professional musician, you probably have more options. As an athlete, you can appear however you want if you are bringing the kind of bottom-line performance that brings victory.

So whether you prefer to show up in a tailored suit or a backwards ball cap, remember, if they can't live without you, your range of choice will expand.

It's also worth noting that if you are not in reasonable physical condition, you may be judged as someone who lacks self-control and discipline. Of course, if you're the kind of person who wants to reach the upper limits of your genetic potential, you're already addressing that.

There is also now a large body of evidence that shows that your body language influences both how others perceive you and how you feel about yourself. If you carry yourself with a strong posture, that's going to affect how others perceive you. Perhaps just as importantly, your own attitude will often reflect the very posture you carry. Just like the mind leads the body, *sometimes the body leads the mind.* So be aware of your posture. Are you slumping? Are you in a contracted position, bent over checking your cell phone? Or are you sitting or standing straight?

While there are some conflicting studies around this, there is evidence that your posture can affect the very hormones your body is producing. If you are in a slumped and contracted position, your cortisol levels rise. Cortisol is a stress hormone that can reduce your confidence and your desire to take risks.

An erect, spread out or "alpha" posture is associated with testosterone, a hormone that breeds confidence. Studies show that you are more likely to take risks when testosterone levels are higher. (That was certainly true on the gridiron.) As such, it makes sense to carry yourself in a more upright and confident manner – or at least to the level that you can. We'll briefly revisit body language in our section on communication. For now, just remember:

Carrying yourself with a strong posture is a critical component when learning to suppress your survival instincts.

3) *What you say*: Have you ever wished you'd just kept your mouth shut? If your answer is yes, it's unanimous. All of us have had moments when we would have been better off just to button it up.

Perhaps more than any other element of control, this should be the easiest. After all, we choose what comes out of our mouths. It's completely up to us and often just a test of our impulse control. But as we know, impulse control is easier said than done.

We all enjoy being right. But sometimes that means we have to make someone else wrong. Making someone else look bad or embarrassing them publicly can come back to haunt us. It rarely ever improves a relationship. As such, sometimes we may want to choose being kind over being right.

Certainly, there are times in business when asserting what you believe is right is essential. The stakes may be high and company money may be on the line. But a good rule to remember is always think first, speak second.

I often tend to think in terms of – *what if I'm being recorded*? As technology becomes more pervasive, we are all subject to being recorded and taped at any time. People act differently when they realize there will be a permanent record of their words or actions.

As a football coach, I echoed Woody Hayes and told my team to practice and play at a level they would be proud of. This "practice the way that you play" became my mantra and it led me to going at full tempo all the time. This kind of "habit formation" can also be useful in how we speak and behave. What if we spoke and behaved as if we were always being taped?

If we believed that there would always be a public record of our activity, we would rarely have to be concerned about saying the wrong thing. Our behavior would improve. Perhaps most importantly, we would develop improved character.

Character is what we do when no one is looking. It is who we are at our core. The good news is that character is not a fixed entity. We can choose to improve it at any moment. When we do, our actions become examples to our friends, family and associates. Our character can then be remembered as a testament to our performance.

We'll dig more deeply into this in our section on communication. For our purposes here, just remember that you are in complete control of your speech.

4) *How you listen to others*: Listening is your most important communication tool. Over 50% of our communication problems result from poor listening. We'll cover this in detail in our next section on communication and influence. For now, just recognize that good listening is an intentional activity that leads to a full understanding of what is being communicated. Without that understanding, problems become inevitable.

5) *What you eat and drink*: What you eat and drink certainly impacts your appearance. Even more importantly, what you eat and drink affects your health. Just like what comes out of your mouth is in your complete control, so is what goes in.

Diabetes, cancer and heart disease are killing us at a far greater rate than terrorism. We are doing this to ourselves. We are literally eating and drinking ourselves to death.

What do we know for sure? We know that sugar, alcohol, fried and processed foods are generally bad for us when taken to excess. They are contributing to obesity and often even hormone imbalances. I'm not suggesting you never enjoy these things. But it's worth taking a look at what you're consuming if you are struggling with your weight and health.

Certainly, with all of the diet programs available, information on nutrition can be confusing. I always recommend choosing a lifestyle that lends itself to healthier eating choices. If you do that, you don't have to get caught up in any particular fad diet. While some of these diets produce great results, it's worth considering the long term. That means choosing a lifestyle over a diet.

What does choosing a lifestyle mean? Essentially it means, I will eat *this* and I won't eat *that*. For you, it might mean choosing to eat fresh vegetables and grass-fed beef or free-range eggs. It might mean going completely vegan. It might mean keeping your eating options open but eliminating products in which any form of sugar is added. Or it might simply mean reducing your calories. You get to choose.

The fact that the diet food industry is a multi-billion-dollar business means that many of us are caught up in the diet craze. It also means that we are spending money that could be spent elsewhere. If my first thought when going on a diet is, "I have to go buy some diet food," – I might need to revisit my underlying nutritional premises.

Healthy options exist everywhere. If you are a person that eats out more often than in, that's fine. Most restaurants have salads and salad bars and a number of healthy selections.

I always say *follow the money*. Consider that no one makes money if you're not buying food and supplements. The food and supplement industries literally bank on you being a consumer. They want to convince you that you're going to be undernourished if you go without their products. Of course, that's not necessarily true.

Here's a thought. Eat less. Simple, I know. But research suggests that you will live longer eating less. You are never told to eat less because no one makes money when you're not eating. If you google "intermittent fasting" you will find some very interesting information on eating protocols. The concept and research behind them are intriguing.

The other thing to be mindful of is to stop eating from boredom or habit. You might be surprised just how much is eaten because it's something to do. We sometimes eat mindlessly while watching television or talking on the phone and we're not even aware we're doing it.

If you struggle with this, you can script your nutrition as part of your daily plan. Schedule when and what you will eat and you can control exactly what you consume. That's why this is considered one of the 13 elements of control.

The bottom line: If you combine eating less with eating healthier, you will be an entirely different person one year from now – and much closer to reaching your ultimate potential.

6) *How often and how intelligently you exercise*: This is another element within our control and it goes hand in hand with nutrition. Like nutrition, there are a wide range of options regarding exercise. How deeply you get into this is simply a reflection of what you want to accomplish.

I believe that weight and strength training give you the greatest return on investment. That is, you get more for 30 minutes to an hour of weight training than any other option. Certainly, cardio exercises for your heart are also valuable. They might include, jogging, cycling, walking, swimming or any activity that elevates your heart into your desired training range. But often, you can elevate your heart with a weight training routine that minimizes rest between sets.

The advantages of weight training are many. I began training with weights before it was a commonly accepted practice. It gave me a competitive advantage that is hard to quantify. But it isn't an overstatement to say that I would not have been nearly as successful as a professional athlete without weight training.

With the muscle mass you gain through training, your body burns more calories even at rest. Your bone density is also increased which becomes increasingly significant as you age. If you consider that there are 168 hours in a week, putting aside four to five hours per week for strength training hardly seems disproportionate.

The beauty of exercise is that it's never too late to begin. I've personally seen men and women take charge of their bodies and transform their health at all ages.

Recognizing that you can find several books and on-line information on how to train, I'm not going to get into the details. However, I want to introduce two concepts. The first is called "the minimum effective dose." The second is called "shock your system."

Occasionally, we are victims of our own enthusiasm. There *is* such a thing as an overuse injury. As a pro athlete, I used to joke that everyone had a certain number of hits that their body could withstand. My number was 237. Unfortunately, I took 352. Humor aside, over the years I've had to become as knowledgeable as a physician to take care of all of the injuries I've incurred. Yet I continue to train and will always be in the best shape that my body will allow.

But overuse becomes an issue as we age. Life accumulates. This can be either positive or negative. When we talk about sports and exercise, there are many activities that accumulate in a positive way. These include conditioning, competition, preparation, execution and planning. But there are also destructive accumulation activities that result in continual deterioration. This is especially true of physical injuries.

Many times, injuries are minor and will heal quickly. But as we get older, the healing process slows down and the previously injured joints and tissue do not recover as quickly. The accumulation of injuries over time can result in major damage.

When I injured my knee on that first day of practice at Ohio State, I had to have surgery and spend significant time in rehabilitation. I continued to injure the knee due to constant collisions with other players and landing on hard surfaces. I always had some inflammation due to the constant trauma. Eventually, I had to have both of my knees replaced with metal joints.

Apart from my own experience, I know several marathoners and triathletes who in their 50's have had at least one hip replacement. Others have had knee issues similar to my own. This is where I advocate for the *"minimum effective dose."*

The minimum effective dose refers to performing enough exercise at the required intensity to stimulate growth or a training effect – and then stopping. It's almost as much art as science. Over time and with experimentation, you begin to understand what your body requires in order to get the proper training effect. Once you master getting the benefits from the minimum effective dose, you do less damage to your body and you can train for more years. You continue to improve while minimizing the creation of unwanted inflammation in the body. In addition, you spend less time at the gym.

But this is key: You must bring enough intensity to your exercise to get the benefit. This brings us to the second concept, *"shock your system."*

Few of us have ever exercised to the point of passing out. Few of us have ever challenged ourselves to the point of full body collapse. Hardcore weight trainers often use concepts such as forced repetitions (where someone assists you once you've exhausted your baseline level of effort) and negative resistance (emphasizing the eccentric movement of the exercise) to effectively shock their systems.

This is as much a mental exercise as a physical one.

Certainly, consult your doctor before beginning an exercise program. If he or she gives you the go-ahead, I recommend that once per week, you take your exercise to the max. *Shock your system*. Find your limit. Test yourself to see how far you can go. Once again, this involves suppressing your survival instinct with the mentality of 100% all-out effort in the moment. Remember, if you've got your physician's go-ahead, your life is not in danger. When you want to quit, it's just your mind trying to protect you.

In order to shock your system, amp yourself up with anger, love, pride, or whatever motivates you. Use whatever your imagination requires. Remember, your mindset and your actions generate emotions. You will find that you can lift heavier weight for many more repetitions than you ever thought possible. *You can always do more*. And each time you do, you will know the joy of being better than you were an hour ago.

If you are applying the *shock your system* concept in the weight room, I recommend having a spotter. This is someone who can assist you in going beyond your perceived capacity – and also someone who can rescue you if by some chance, you *do* take yourself to complete body collapse.

Certainly, you can test your cardio limits as well. Once you realize that you have significant command over your body's health and appearance, you begin to get a sense of empowerment and control that you can apply to every area of your life.

Have you ever shocked your system in your day-to-day life?

For example, how about business? What if once a week, you pushed yourself to work overtime? What if you stayed up three hours later to finish a project? What if you got up an hour earlier every day to read something worthwhile?

Shocking your system is like swimming upstream against the current. It's easy to swim with the current. It's easy to go with the flow and do everything that everyone else does. That's the definition of mediocrity. That's not us.

We are talking about suppressing our very survival instincts. Once again, we are talking about being unreasonable. We are talking about taking the path of *most* resistance!

Shocking your system in everyday life simply means that you perform the action that is causing the resistance. What is the thing that needs to be done? *Do that thing!*

Go against the grain. Make that difficult phone call. Have that difficult conversation. Get up earlier and stay up later. Order the healthy option at the restaurant. Write those thank you notes.

Stop procrastinating.

Ask yourself what 100% actually looks like in whatever task you're performing. Once you begin the practice of shocking your system, it becomes a habit. It becomes easier because you actually see the amazing benefits that you reap. You see the proof that you are far more capable than you suspected.

7) *Your education and what you read*: There is no question that the cost of a college education has skyrocketed. It's a very real and often daunting expense. Yet people of all incomes and all circumstances are finding a way. Affordable on-line colleges that enable distance learning are becoming more popular and allowing people to work while going to school. Whatever path you're on and no matter your age, I encourage everyone, when possible, to get a college education because it provides credentials and opens doors into professions that are honorable and worthwhile.

Having said this, college is just one method of becoming educated. After college, I realized that I still needed more education to be successful. I was a professional athlete with a limited shelf life in the NFL as a player. I immediately began networking and meeting people that were outside the world of athletics. I realized that a career in the NFL would not last long.

But having recently graduated from Ohio State University, I did not want to dedicate the time, effort or expense to increase my knowledge with another degree. Instead, I decided to pursue specific licenses that would allow me to obtain expertise in the areas I wanted to pursue. It began with a real estate license. In four weeks, I was able to take a course and pass the state license requirements for real estate.

Shortly afterward, I took a course and passed the state requirements for a general contractor. After that, I attended classes and passed the state requirements to obtain a security's license and a mortgage loan license. These licenses allowed me to participate in each of these occupations without enduring the cost and time of attending a college or university.

The course schedules were intense and reflected actual real-life cases of professionals involved in these lines of work. The instructors were professionals, each licensed in their specific field and not career teachers. I was able to learn how these various industries operated and what would be required to be successful as an individual licensee. By studying actual transactions, I was able to learn faster and recall specific cases that impacted the industry. It is truly amazing what you can learn from the expertise of industry professionals, in addition to the mistakes that others have made. These classes have made a huge difference in my life after football.

Fortunately, it has never been easier to get information. Free on-line tutorial services such as Kahn Academy offer education to anyone with a desire to learn. The Internet gives us access to immediate answers that thirty years ago only existed in out-of-date encyclopedias. The world is literally at our fingertips.

I hope that more schools bring back vocational training for those with that kind of aptitude. Wood, metal and machine shop classes would be very useful for many of our young people. We don't live in a "one size fits all" universe.

Books exist on-line and also in hard and paperback forms. They are phenomenal learning tools and you can choose from whatever genre of books you want.

The bottom line is simply that you are accountable for your education. In today's world, there are no excuses for not knowing what you need to know.

8) *The people who surround you*: Remember YAWYAW? You are who you associate with. There is no need to belabor this. Just remember that it is largely within your control. Yes, I understand that you sometimes have to associate with colleagues or even family members who are not elevating your performance. But when it's up to you, choose to be around people who elevate your game.

9) *The news you consume*: From where do you get your news? Television? Radio? Newspaper? On-line? Whatever your answer, you get to choose. It might be worth considering trying to get news from a variety of sources if only to get a broader range of perspectives.

In the same way that the people you surround yourself with influence you, the news you consume shapes the way that you think, what you believe and who you become. In life, it's good to have options. Take advantage of a variety of news sources and recognize that news sources exist because they can sell advertising dollars. Those who control those dollars may have a large say in what news gets presented and how. Therefore, be vigilant in what you see, hear and read. Attempt to understand how it impacts your perspective. This allows you to think independently and use your best judgment. Be a discerning information consumer.

Remember, simply consuming information isn't necessarily the same thing as being informed.

10) *How you treat people and the success of your relationships*: This might seem like a no-brainer but we sometimes live on autopilot. We forget to be mindful of how we are treating the people closest to us, our loved ones and colleagues.

We unintentionally sabotage relationships by taking people for granted, or we simply forget our manners. Strong, aware people are polite. Weak and insecure people are rude. All of these behaviors are completely within our control.

We can make it a habit to take charge of our relationships. We can take ownership of how meaningful and productive they are. We can catch people doing something right and compliment them. We can take extra time with our children, listening to them and helping them along their path. These things seem practically cliché yet they require our attention and they require that we take action.

I once overheard a somewhat humorous question posed by a psychologist to a client: *If your relationships are bad, and you're always there, who do you think might be at fault?*

The psychologist was simply suggesting that his client was the common denominator in all of his relationships. So by examining his own role in his relationship outcomes, the client might be able to improve them.

Simply reaching out and making the first gesture of love and care can transform a relationship. Again, like all of these elements of control, it's our choice.

11) *How you spend your time*: How you spend your time is the clearest reflection of your values and priorities. If you say that health is your greatest value, but you never exercise or eat healthy, you're not really valuing it.

You can get directly in touch with your most important values simply by examining what you do every day. You might be shocked to find out that what you thought was really important, in reality, isn't. Many people are also shocked to find out how much time they spend watching television, talking on the phone, or looking at social media. These are often referred to as the "electronic income reducers."

If the things you're doing are not enhancing your life, ask yourself, "What am I willing to give up in order to be great?"

Consider creating a "stop doing" list. Where are you wasting time? You don't have to major in minor things once you stop to consider how you actually use time.

If you're not spending time on the things that you say are significant, why is that? Only you can answer that. The important takeaway here is simply that you get to choose. Taking control of your time brings us back to your daily script. Scheduling how you spend your time takes temptation and random chance out of the picture. If something is important to you, put it into your plan. Commit it to paper. Then do it whether or not you feel like it.

That's what professionals do.

12) *Where you spend your time*: If you're down at the local tavern every night after work, it says something about you. If you're at the library or the gym, that says something. If you're at your child's soccer game or home in front of the television; that says something as well.

Just like *how* you spend your time, *where* you spend your time speaks volumes. When you take control of the places you frequent, you help take control of your success.

13) *Your income*: We addressed this at the beginning of this section. All you need to remember is that if you can provide a service or product that people are willing to pay for – and they refuse to live without it – you will generate wealth.

I challenge you to examine the thirteen elements above. Grade yourself on how well you are handling each one. Your personal brand is largely reflected by how you manage these elements. It pays to be brutally honest with yourself. No one has to see your answers.

It will take some time and introspection to examine these elements. It will require personal discipline. But personal discipline provides the foundation for all achievement. Look at the undisciplined people you know. How are their lives working out?

Look at the people who never accept responsibility for their behavior or their results. How about their lives; how is it going for them? Unless they were born with a silver spoon in their mouth, they are probably struggling.

How about you. Do you beat everyone to the office each day? Do you stay later? Do you take on extra responsibilities and tasks that others are unwilling to do? You are in control of the answers to these questions. Yes, I understand you may have to pick up the kids at daycare or school. I understand that like everyone, you have personal commitments that must be handled. But it's ultimately on you to figure out how to navigate all of the issues in your life in order to add value within your circumstances.

No matter in what situation you find yourself, the thirteen elements above are relevant. You may be young and strong. You may be in a wheelchair. You may be a heart patient or a cancer survivor. From wherever you sit or stand, you are in charge of how you handle these thirteen elements of control.

Taking on this accountability mindset is important. Why?

Because *no one is coming to save you.*

You may have noticed a proliferation of superhero movies in the culture today. While entertaining, these movies feed a cultural fantasy that someone is coming to the rescue. Taking on an extreme accountability mindset enables you to rescue yourself. And when you're rescuing yourself, you're not being a burden to others.

Cultivating this mindset will make you an outlier and completely differentiate you from most people in the United States today. Unlike so many others, you will not be declaring yourself a victim. You will be taking charge of your circumstances and taking the actions necessary to dominate your life and environment.

This level of accountability leads you directly into the final component of our "A" game…

Accomplishment

Victory.

Winning.

Achievement.

Closing the deal.

Whatever you call it, accomplishing whatever you set out to do feels great. It is the final component of our "A" game. It drives us and makes us want more.

But interestingly, people remember defeat more than victory. If you examine history, most success is built upon the ashes of defeat. Yet only a certain segment of the population bothers to get up after defeat. That's why adopting the "46 Attack Mindset" is essential to living a life that is not wasted in the pain of regret.

Under the shadow of adversity, we find out what we're made of. We find out who we really are. Some of us fight; some of us flee; some of us freeze.

Those who adopt the "46 Attack Mindset" recognize the situation they're in and get right to work on a solution. Time spent dwelling on the problem, unless it's to get a better understanding of the difficulty, is wasted. After a defeat, "A gamers" use the loss to fuel the fire that gets them right back into the game. They bring a consistently competitive attitude to everything they do.

Sometimes their competitive drive comes from what is commonly called "a chip on the shoulder." This refers to the idea that the competitor has been slighted or disrespected in some fashion. They use this perceived slight, whether real or imaginary, to give them extra motivation.

If I ever had a chip on my shoulder, it was only because I was labeled as too small, too slow or too inexperienced to make it at the highest level of professional sports. Certainly, I wanted to prove that assessment wrong. But honestly, I was self-motivated. I didn't need anyone else's opinion to drive me.

I will, however, point out that I got a great sense of satisfaction when Joe Paterno, as cited earlier in the book, said that not offering Doug Plank a scholarship to Penn State was a big mistake. What I had not realized was that Joe often used me as an example that the value of a player can't always be evaluated from the outside. I found out about this when I was approached by an assistant coach at Penn State as I was being inducted into a Pennsylvania State Hall of Fame.

That felt good.

But I was always motivated from within. From Pee Wee football to the Chicago Bears, I was lit up to go all-out every time. It didn't hurt that I loved contact. As a youngster, I remember the thrill of being rewarded as an aggressive hitter. Not everyone is wired that way. As we've learned, most people shy away from collisions as part of their instinct to survive. But as we are discovering, by learning to control our minds, we can overcome instincts that don't serve us.

Our daily lives are not typically characterized by actual collisions. However, our daily lives *are* characterized by the reality of competition. This competition can seem like a collision that we want to avoid. But bringing your "A" game means to love competition because it makes you better. It forces you to improve.

It's also important to recognize that at the end of competition is where accomplishment lives.

Our creative juices are most often driven from competition. Certainly, there are exceptions. Sometimes we just feel the need to express ourselves in some creative way. But even within such altruistic fields as medicine, many breakthroughs are achieved because there is a race to get a cure to the market. Competition drives progress. Whether we are talking about medicine, communication, or travel, being the first with the best brings the most reward.

In a world of competition, the "46 Attack Mindset" advocates using whatever ethical competitive advantage you can find. You want to maximize your strengths and exploit your competition's weaknesses. In football, we attempted to exploit matchups. As such, we were always looking for the other team's weak link.

While with the Bears, I played with an extraordinary defensive lineman named Dan Hampton. Dan was quick, strong and tough. Offensive linemen found him almost impossible to block. To maximize our competitive advantage, we would move Dan around in order to match him up against the opposition's weakest blocker. When doing this, he was practically unstoppable.

We actually saw other teams move their weakest lineman to other positions in order to avoid lining up against Dan. It was almost comical. Between Dan's domination at his position and the aggressive nature of the 46 defense, we had a distinct competitive advantage.

You can exploit matchups in business as well. For example, you always want your best and most experienced presenters pitching to your most important clients. Too often, because of scheduling or travel conflicts, the office rookie gets thrown to the wolves and revenues get lost as a result. You always want to put people in a position to win.

You can do this by understanding your team's strengths and weaknesses. Then find out what motivates them. Train them. Help them develop a plan to improve because your team is only as strong as its weakest member.

Most importantly, help them learn to think as if they owned the business and reward them when they do. Use every parcel of information that you can gather to help everyone succeed.

When I owned fast food franchises, we continually worked to reward both customers *and* employees. We'll examine this more closely in our section on communication and influence. For now, just recognize that your business will flourish when you actually address the needs and motivations of all the stakeholders in your business. Employees, customers and suppliers all play a vital role in the success of any business. There is a direct relationship with the lowest paid employee and the attitude of your company.

In addition to your stakeholders, it's also useful to know as much as possible about your competitors. Where are they outperforming you? How are they doing it? What might you be able to change to gain a competitive advantage?

Once you understand the strengths and weaknesses of your competition, you once again employ the "46 Attack Mindset." What does that mean?

It means it's time to make the competition worry about you!

By now, you understand that when we employ the "46" – we don't react. We act. We get off first. We focus on what we do well. This forces the competition to react to us.

This aggressive approach to being the first and the best with the highest quality is a lifelong pursuit. And it relates to everything you do, personally and professionally. Accomplishment never needs to end. You can always improve and grow, even with limitations. Striving to make the best of what you have is the key to accomplishment…

And it is the essence of reaching the upper limits of your genetic potential.

———

One last word about accomplishment.

You may have noticed a number of distinctions being made throughout the book. For example; 1) being a player versus being a spectator, 2) the pain of execution versus the pain of regret, 3) action versus inaction and 4) being aggressive versus being passive. Here is yet another distinction to consider.

It's important to make a distinction between celebrity and accomplishment. There are people out there who are famous simply because they've learned how to be a celebrity. In essence, that's their only achievement.

They've not cured cancer. They've not discovered a breakthrough technology nor have they created a great work of art. They have simply learned how to garner attention. As such, they get a number of social media hits.

This is relatively harmless until you consider that, when asking young people what they want to be when they grow up, we seldom hear doctor, lawyer, firefighter, professional athlete, teacher or police officer.

What we overwhelmingly hear is, "Famous. I want to be famous."

We rarely hear about contributing to the community's greater good. We don't hear about sacrificing in service for a greater cause.

Attention, in conjunction with money, has become the most valued currency.

I only make this distinction to bring awareness to the fact that perhaps we can begin to use the currency of attention to better reward those who actually produce valuable goods and services. In our businesses, we can shine a greater light on those who make the sacrifices that bring success to themselves and others. We can reward our children when they bring home better grades and put out more effort. We can appeal to the emotions of those who otherwise might squander great gifts.

Emotions are what drive us. They turbo-charge the engine that propels us into action. How we take charge of those emotions and use them to influence ourselves and others will be the focus of our next section.

DOUG PLANK

MVP of my high school conference as a Quarterback.

**NFL legend, George Blanda, inspired me with the belief that I
could achieve athletic success beyond high school**

One Hit – One Knockout

Just another day at the office

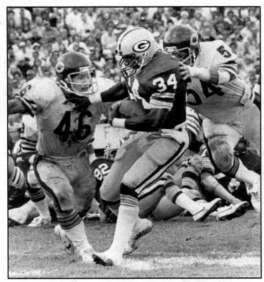

I had to go all-out 100% of the time

With my friend, mentor, and former coach, the great Mike Ditka

With the legend, Walter Payton, and Chicago Mayor Jane Byrne

With two Chicago icons, Harry Caray and Doug Buffone

I learned a lot from Buddy Ryan

After football, my very first fast-food franchise

**Life is precious – I rolled my vehicle eight times and
crawled out the blood-stained window**

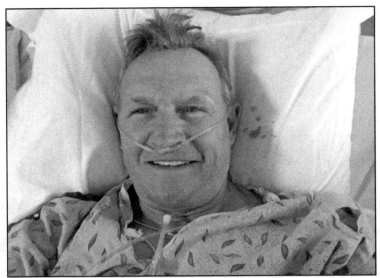

Grateful to be alive after the accident

Another view of the vehicle

Coaching required energy, enthusiasm and communication skills

Speaking after receiving the Arena League Coach of the Year award in 2007

SECTION TWO: Communication and Influence

Chapter Three – Deliver the Message:
An Arrow Straight to the Heart

Whether you're on the football field or the battle field; whether you're in the boardroom or in a relationship, success comes down to how you choose to manage and own yourself in the moment.

Doug Plank

We had just suffered a tough loss to the San Francisco 49ers. The loss was primarily due to our poor play on defense.

Sitting with my teammates, we watched as our defensive coordinator, Buddy Ryan, walked to the front of the room. Buddy had been a master sergeant in the Korean War and that's just how he treated us. He told us exactly what he thought of us, as players, and sometimes as people. No holds barred.

At this point, Buddy was still relatively new to the Chicago Bear organization. Because of his strict and gruff manner, he had not made many friends and he was not particularly popular. We sat in silence waiting for what we assumed would be the stereotypical loud critique of a poor performance. When things went badly, that's what most of us had experienced throughout our years of playing football.

We got something else entirely.

Quietly, Buddy said, "I expect most of you in this room to make mistakes. I expect that most of you can't always be counted on. But there is a handful of you in here that I count on, that I rely on."

He paused before continuing, "I respect your ability and I need you to do what I ask you to do. When that doesn't happen, I don't handle it very well as a coach."

We then watched as Buddy stared off into oblivion. After what seemed like minutes, tears started rolling down his face.

At that moment, I truly believe that the Chicago Bears became the "Monsters of the Midway." From then on, to a man, whatever Buddy wanted from that group, he was going to get.

There's a common saying in football…*players don't care how much you know until they know how much you care.*

We now knew how much Buddy cared. It mattered to him and we understood that he was completely invested in us. As a result, we were now completely invested in him. From that moment forward, that defensive unit would do anything for Buddy Ryan.

Great success was to follow.

———

If overcoming adversity is the number one key to success, effective communication is the navigational tool that can get you there. Successful communication provides the foundation for accomplishment and creates the opportunity to impact others.

In sports, effective communication allows coaches, players and fans to interact with emotion. A properly delivered pregame speech will provide energy and focus for the players. Sometimes it's the difference between winning and losing.

On the other hand, a poorly delivered message will result in lack of effort or poor execution. Years ago, while operating a Burger King restaurant, I asked the dining room hostess to check the bathrooms. A short time later, a customer came to the front counter and told us that the men's bathroom was filthy and needed attention. I immediately asked the hostess if she had checked the bathrooms. She said, "Yes, I checked the bathrooms and they are filthy."

I hadn't specifically asked her to report back to me or fix the problem. So poor communication on my part resulted in a bad experience for a customer. The lesson? Be specific and direct.

Buddy Ryan understood the power of specific and direct communication. Even more importantly, he was able to use genuine emotion while also eliciting great peer pressure to move his organization. Always authentic and real, he was a master at pushing people's buttons. With this ability to influence, he got the best out of his players.

Buddy created a system that wasn't as much about your position as it was about your disposition. By the time Buddy was done talking with you, you would do anything not to disappoint him or your teammates.

When he opened up to us after the 49er game, we began to see that Buddy was more than just a gruff drill sergeant. He was a genuine human being who could move us from tears to laughter in just a matter of moments. In truth, he was a master manipulator.

Now you may think of "manipulation" as some kind of devious Machiavellian concept used to advance someone's personal agenda. It's true that some people attempt to manipulate others for personal gain. But manipulation is simply another word for influence. And if you can influence or manipulate human beings to maximize their potential and contribute to the common good, that's a benefit to all. Everyone wins.

How did Buddy do it?

Buddy never used names. If you were in his favor, he called you by your number. If you were in his doghouse, he would call you by an unsavory and colorful adjective or noun. This depersonalization had an element of humor to it but it also seemed to make us more accountable to one another. It eliminated any idea that Buddy was playing favorites or that any "prima donna" behavior would be tolerated. No one got "star treatment" and everyone was dealt with equally and fairly.

Calling us by numbers instead of names might not have worked except for the fact that *we knew Buddy cared*. Behind the gruff exterior was the soul of a man who would do anything for us. Buddy was in the trenches with us. He became like a stern father figure.

There was always a method to Buddy's madness and truly, he made playing defense fun. He was both aggressive *and* progressive! He took risks, tried different schemes and made each of us understand our role in the overall success of the unit. Rather than impose a particular defensive system on us, he looked at our individual potential and adapted his defense to our talents.

For example, he knew that I was one of the unit's better tacklers so he brought me closer to the line of scrimmage in the 46 defense. Our cornerbacks were great one-on-one pass coverage guys so we trusted them to handle the wide receivers on their own. Buddy's willingness to study and exploit our strengths made us even more eager to buy in to what he wanted.

While often complicated in theory, Buddy would always try to simplify his defensive schemes for us. In the service of clear communication, he used the chalkboard to tell us what to do. He then took us out onto the field to show us and demonstrate what to do. Then on game day, he empowered us to go do it.

More than anything, Buddy built in a system of accountability and loyalty to one another. We would do anything not to disappoint our teammates or Buddy. In the middle of a game, if I made a mistake, fell down or missed an assignment, I can remember thinking, *what is this going to look like on film tomorrow? I better get up and hit somebody now! An opponent, a teammate, an official, anybody – but hit something!*

This feeling of accountability was perhaps the greatest communication lesson I took from Buddy Ryan. He taught us that if you build in a system of accountability to one another – and you genuinely care about your people and the outcome – your likelihood of success will increase dramatically.

More than anything, Buddy used emotion and showed that he cared.

We responded accordingly.

————

In the last chapter, we talked about how we would use our outstanding defensive lineman, Dan Hampton, to exploit matchups. This was just one aspect of another of Buddy Ryan's winning strategies. Buddy understood the power of intimidation.

You might not think of intimidation as a form of communication. But if someone is intimidating you, they are communicating power, force and an aura of overwhelming capability that makes you change what you are doing. That is certainly a way to communicate – and Buddy Ryan was the master of it.

Buddy's 46 defense was all about intimidation. We could literally see the fear in a quarterback's eyes as he called the signals. He knew that if he didn't get his pass off in less than 1.5 seconds, guys named Hampton, Dent, McMichael, Wilson, and yes, Plank, were going to have a meeting right where he stood. We became like sharks in a feeding frenzy.

Moving Hampton around to line up against their worst blocker was a featured component of Buddy's intimidation strategy. We always wanted our best against their worst. Buddy called this, "Looking for Susie."

Every team has a Susie. This is the player that does not love contact and aggression. This is the guy that doesn't look at inflicting pain as part of the job description. When we found the opposing team's Susie, Buddy instructed Hampton to move over across from him just before the ball was snapped. When other teams tried to move that lineman away from him, Hampton would find him and the disruption to the offense was maximized.

This is a perfect example of the strength of a chain. A team is comprised of links – and they are only as strong as their weakest link. A team's strength is not measured by how strong the strongest player is, but instead by the strength of their weakest one. Buddy could always find the Susie in the opposition.

Intimidation as a communication strategy may seem cold-hearted. But in the world of business and sports, if the competition fears you, you have the upper hand. As the "46 Attack Mindset" suggests, *always make them adjust to you.*

———

Our time with Buddy Ryan was not without humor. Used properly, humor can be a very important communication tool. If you can tie an important message to humor, people will more readily remember it.

In my last year as a Bear, we were playing the Dallas Cowboys on Thanksgiving Day. I was having a really good day. I had two sacks on safety blitzes, an interception, and had put some good licks on their running backs and receivers.

But, as sometimes happened, on one of those hits I suffered a mild concussion. I also cracked two ribs. This made it incredibly painful to even breathe. It also impacted my ability to tackle because I couldn't wrap my arms around the ball carrier.

Late in the game, we were leading. The Cowboys had the ball with less than a minute left and they were driving for what would be the winning score. They were on our 20-yard line. It was third down and they needed five yards for a first down.

Their quarterback, Danny White, dropped back to pass but instead, handed the ball to their All-Pro running back, Tony Dorsett, on a draw play. Dorsett paused momentarily, and then ran through a small hole at the line of scrimmage.

After initially taking a step back to protect against a pass, I began running forward as fast as I could. I hit Dorsett in the chest with my helmet and drove him back five yards. But I didn't knock him off his feet and because of the excruciating pain in my ribs, I couldn't wrap him up to make the tackle. Being the great back that he was, he managed to maintain his balance and continued running for the winning touchdown.

Walking off the field, I knew what I was in for. I heard Buddy yelling and screaming. He ran up to me and grabbed me by the facemask. As he peppered me with some colorful expletives, he stared right into my eyes and finally said, "Blondie, the Chicago Bears are paying you $100,000 to tackle that son of a bitch!"

I thought about it for a moment and replied, "You're right Buddy. The Bears *are* paying me $100,000 to tackle every running back. But do you realize, the Cowboys are paying Tony Dorsett a million dollars to go around me?"

It was one of the few times anyone ever saw Buddy Ryan speechless.

———

No matter what your occupation, your success will depend upon your ability to communicate clearly and succinctly. At crunch time, your words will need to convey the necessary knowledge and ideas with the appropriate sense of urgency and passion.

American history is replete with examples of U.S. Presidents that moved the nation with their words. From Lincoln's Gettysburg Address to Kennedy's "Ask not what your country can do for you," words convey ideals and move people to action.

When I look back at my own life, I can remember what people said to me even more than what they did. Each of us can remember something said to us during our lives that had a profound effect on our behavior, feelings and memories – for good or for ill.

With our own ability to communicate, we each have the power to move mountains. The quote at the beginning of this chapter speaks to how we manage and own ourselves in the moment. This requires incredible self-awareness and a recognition that *the next thing out of your mouth could either heal, hurt, motivate, or destroy.*

The success of your marriage, your occupation, and personal relationships are determined by your ability to reach out and touch someone with your words. But you must own and manage yourself in the moment in order to say the appropriate thing.

Here is a clear example of the impact of an ill-timed phrase. I can remember being just nine years old and striking out to end a Little League baseball game. On the drive home, my father asked me, "Doug, why did you strike out?"

What kind of a question is that? I was nine years old and for heaven's sakes, I didn't purposely strike out! This happened over a half-century ago yet I remember it like it was yesterday. That's the destructive power of a thoughtless and hurtful comment. Over the years, I've learned a lot about what *not* to do from how people have treated me.

On the other hand, there have been many times when people have been incredibly gracious and thoughtful with their words.

In another game against the 49ers, San Francisco was driving for what would be the winning touchdown if they scored. Time was winding down and Quarterback Steve DeBerg was looking for his tight end up the seam. I read the play, anticipated the throw and made a leaping interception to effectively end the game.

The following week, the Bear offensive coordinator, Ted Marchibroda, made a point of coming over to me to say thanks. He said, "You saved the game for us. Your interception was the difference."

Now this wouldn't have been such a big deal but the coordinators on either side of the ball rarely spoke to the other unit's players. For that matter, getting that kind of a compliment rarely happened to any of us. The fact that Ted Marchibroda had an impressive NFL pedigree made me even more proud.

Ted had previously led the Baltimore Colts to three division championships and been an offensive innovator, introducing such concepts as the no-huddle offense. Ted ended up spending six decades in pro football. During his time, he had been a quarterback, an offensive coordinator, head coach and broadcaster. He even gave legendary New England coach, Bill Belichick, his first NFL job as a Baltimore assistant when Bill was just 23 years old.

But more than anything, Ted Marchibroda was a classy human being. I have never forgotten his kindness.

———

As I look back, my life has been punctuated by gracious moments that I remember because of their positive impact.

For a time, I lived in Atlanta, working as a head coach for the Georgia Force in the Arena League and as an assistant with the Falcons. Eventually I moved to take a job with the New York Jets but before doing so, I wrote a nice letter to the iconic Atlanta Falcons owner, Arthur Blank. Arthur also owned the Force.

Arthur had begun building his fortune in 1978 as co-founder of Home Depot. He was a very successful and busy man. For all I knew, he might not even see my letter. But I wanted to say thank you for the opportunities he had afforded me. I did not expect a response; I simply wanted to express my genuine and heartfelt appreciation.

A year later, I was coaching with the Jets and we were preparing to play the Falcons at the Meadowlands. I was talking with another coach on the sideline before the game. All of a sudden, the coach grabbed me and said, "Hey Doug, look! That's Arthur Blank and he's walking this way. I wonder who he wants to see."

I wondered as well and we both looked around to see if there were any notable people that Arthur might want to talk with. As it turned out, it was me. Arthur walked over, happy to see me and thanked me for the kind letter I had sent. He was very appreciative and my visit with him taught me a lesson. The simple act of expressing thanks can never be underestimated.

When was the last time you took a moment to share a sincere compliment or note of thanks?

You never know the impact of your kind words.

———

When I say the words "Mike Ditka," what do you think of?

I'll bet you think of toughness. The old NFL films that show him breaking tackles, stiff-arming defenders and refusing to go down are some of my favorite clips. They define his all-out aggressive and hard-hitting competitive style. Mike Ditka was truly old-school.

Very few people know that Mike and former Oakland Raider quarterback and coach, Tom Flores, are the only people who have ever won NFL titles as a player, an assistant coach and a head coach. But when Mike took over as head coach of the Bears, we all knew his history. As a player, he was one of the first tight ends in the NFL who became a threat as both a pass receiver and a blocker. He truly helped to define the tight end position as we know it today.

But here is something a lot of people don't know about Mike. Because he was such a tough guy, people don't often give Mike enough credit as a strategist and teacher. Mike Ditka was a very effective communicator.

Before Mike, many of my prior NFL coaches spoke like cemetery directors. They had a lot of people underneath them but no one was listening.

Mike Ditka was the exact opposite. He would put a message on a verbal arrow and shoot it straight into your heart. He captivated every room he walked into. He was like the Ronald Reagan of coaches in communication. He painted a picture of exactly what you needed to do. Even today, when he speaks, he speaks plainly, honestly and directly. He leaves nothing to chance.

I remember Mike's first team meeting as head coach of the Bears. He immediately began laying down the law.

He said, "There's a new sheriff in town. If you are early, you are on time. If you are on time, you are late."

This was Mike showing us that discipline was going to be enforced and that we had better expect some changes. In fact, Mike provided us with much needed discipline and he outlined the plan to get the Bears to the Super Bowl. He set clear expectations and coached like he played – all out. No one could convey the idea of "us versus them" like Mike Ditka.

Mike also taught us that hustle will always beat talent when talent does not hustle. As such, he would not tolerate anything less than 100% effort. That completely resonated with me and I lived it every day.

At that very first team meeting, Mike explained that some of us would not be around the following year. He explained that a team is only as strong as its weakest link – and the weak links would be removed. He never pulled punches.

Mike Ditka was a very powerful leader.

———

In my life, I have found three types of coaches and bosses. I call them Aspirin, Penicillin, and Chemo.

Aspirin coaches make minor pains go away for a short time. But these coaches lack communication skills and they don't do the work necessary to acquire competent players or assistant coaches. In fact, they are afraid to hire an assistant coach who might be talented enough to replace them.

Aspirin coaches are like that cemetery director who have a great many people underneath them, but no one is listening.

Penicillin coaches can cure most of the issues that affect a team. They are good at instilling hope and taking care of basic problems. But they do not have the personality to overcome serious internal problems inside of an organization. They can't cure cancer on a team. Cancer shows up in negative attitudes, lack of effort, and general internal unrest within the organization. You can see it every year in the NFL. Players openly contest decisions made and there is often turmoil on the staff and even the front office.

Only Chemo coaches can cure cancer. Chemo coaches are confident, demanding and great communicators. They are smart but they don't act like professors. They usually have a charismatic personality and the ability to communicate clearly and effectively.

Chemo coaches have personally faced adversity and conflict in their own lives. As such, they usually have an understanding of what's going wrong. The problem is, the team can't stay on chemo for too long. The Chemo coach must be able to adapt and make the necessary adjustments or the team will die.

Chemo coaches and leaders who can adapt are in high demand today because business leaders and NFL coaches are facing many of the same communication issues. They have a younger work force coming into their organizations who are more mobile, more technology-savvy, and quite honestly, more easily distracted by all of the information coming their way.

These young people are generally very talented and it is essential that they be handled properly. They are very bright but unlike their parents and grandparents, they are used to instant gratification. And why wouldn't they be? They can order something online and have it at their house the next day. They can reach out to anyone and communicate instantly. They can find out the answer to any question almost immediately from their cell phone.

As business leaders and coaches, it will help us to see things from the younger person's perspective. They are not going to be as patient when waiting for a promotion. They are not going to be as tolerant waiting for a "choice" assignment that can make a difference to the organization. They have rarely had to wait for anything and they are always looking for the next thing that might be better.

This isn't necessarily bad news if you know what you're dealing with. So what do we do?

We practice the most important communication skill. We practice the lost art of listening.

Listening

Obviously, we can't give our younger work force everything they want immediately. But we can value their input by truly listening to them. Our young people want to be respected and leaders can demonstrate that respect by genuinely hearing what they have to say. And having heard them, we can work with them to develop a plan that shows them that, if they perform to the standards we set, we can help them advance.

This willingness and ability to listen is completely consistent with the "46 Attack Mindset." Why? Because it's easier to aggressively go after what you want when you have the best information to work with.

As we mentioned when covering our "13 Elements of Control," over 50% of communication problems are the result of poor listening. Think about that. That means that if you make a practice of listening better and improving your moment-to-moment attention, you could dramatically improve your business and personal relationships. Too many people listen in order to reply instead of understand.

Proper listening skills help to build a culture of respect within teams and organizations. Taking the time to actually hear and examine input builds rapport and establishes a bond with the speaker. In addition, it will save you time trying to find answers. If people are not rewarded for sharing information, they tend to withhold it. Then, as a leader, you must waste valuable time trying to dig for data.

The most progressive companies around the world encourage listening to their employees. Whether using suggestion boxes or employee surveys, the best companies solicit input. But having gathered the input, they *must* act on it. If they don't at least acknowledge that they've heard the employees or customers, they are worse off than never having asked in the first place.

The lesson? *You reinforce people's willingness to share by actually valuing the information they give.*

In a culture where texting, instant messaging and faster communication protocols are the rule, the lost art of listening can save time, money and heartache. After all, the people closest to the action in the workplace are the ones most familiar with the operation. Whether it's the mechanic on the factory floor or the office administrator fielding and distributing sales calls, these folks often have the best answers to problems because they are right in the middle of the battle. We need to hear them.

This is why so many companies have gone to a morning huddle. Often called a "standup meeting," these brief gatherings bring teams together to cover daily assignments and review progress each morning. They also give everyone the opportunity to relay new information or call an audible that could impact the operation.

Just like a play call in a football huddle, these standup business huddles make sure everyone is on the same page, clear on their tasks and moving in the same direction.

Now that we've covered the importance of listening, let's take a deeper look into doing it more effectively.

———

Have you ever considered that you have a talking to listening ratio? In daily conversations, experts suggest that if you are talking 40 percent of the time and listening 60 percent of the time, you are probably doing well. We shouldn't be too hard on ourselves when we violate this because there are times when our passion for a subject simply takes over. But generally, if we are to improve our comprehension, we should speak less and listen more.

If you really think about it, we're trained from a young age not to listen. As kids, we hear the threats from our parents, "Don't do that or you'll be sent to your room!" Typically, two or three threats like that occur before any consequences take place, if they ever do. We learn to tune it all out.

Parents who are the most successful communicators typically get down on eye level with their child and speak very calmly and deliberately. "Look at me and listen very closely. I need you to pick up your toys and put them away. If you do not, you will be going to bed immediately."

That strategy is usually better in teaching children to listen, particularly if the parent follows through with consequences when appropriate.

The reason I raise this issue is because by the time many of us have entered the world of business, we are trained to be poor listeners. That fact, along with all of the various media competing for our attention, makes us even less attentive.

The solution lies in a desire to get better. There are certain strategies we can employ to improve our listening skills. But most importantly, we need to be aware of our problem and have a strong desire to improve.

Here are some listening practices you can put into place:

1) To better get a sense of your listening to talking ratio, try going to a week of meetings and saying nothing unless you are making a presentation or asked a question. Take notes on what you hear and really focus on the content of what people are saying. Are they saying what they really mean? Are their actions consistent with their words? How do you feel just listening and not speaking? If you feel frustrated, consider what that might say about your own need to be heard – and then consider how others feel when not allowed to contribute.

   Towards the end of the week, give yourself permission to ask questions in case you want to gather more information. Assess yourself as a listener and resolve to continue practicing your present-moment listening awareness.

2) To avoid confusion or misinterpretation, ask the speaker to be specific. If they are giving instructions, be sure to find out exactly what they need, when they need it, and how they want to receive it, whether it's information, a product or a written report. Repeat back to them what you heard and always make yourself the responsible party to ensure clear communication.

3) To ensure that you get everything the speaker is saying, make a point of focusing on the first words they say. This will speed up your point of contact

as a listener. If they are in the room with you, turn to face them. Make them the most important thing in the moment.

4) If you initially find yourself disagreeing with the speaker, don't automatically tune out. Stay open and attempt to understand the person's point of view. Always allow them to finish their thought. Hearing another person's perspective gives us another opportunity to learn.

5) A short pen is better than a long memory. When possible, write important points down if you will need to remember them later.

The bottom line: Those who adopt the "46 Attack Mindset" listen with intent to understand. They stay mindful of the "listen 60 percent and speak 40 percent" rule and remain open minded to several points of view.

Qualities of a Great Speaker

Whether addressing a football team before a game or speaking to colleagues at a professional convention, great communicators share certain common qualities.

It's no secret that many people fear public speaking. Surveys tell us that they often rate it to be more terrifying than death, which ironically, means people would rather be dead than giving the eulogy.

Irony aside, those surveys give us a perfect real-world example of where people trick themselves into thinking they are in a survival situation – when in reality, they're not. We know that in order to suppress our survival instinct, we need to take control of our mind. In this instance, it means taking charge of the first of four qualities that make a great speaker.

1) Be Prepared – Overcoming the fear of public speaking is often simply a matter of being ready. Researching your topic to the point of being an expert will eliminate a good percentage of whatever frightens you. *This is something you control.* Is it easy? No. Does it take time? Yes.

   Unless you have been asked to give an impromptu, spur-of-the-moment speech, you should take whatever time you need to be prepare. That shows respect for your audience and respect for your own career and personal development. Audiences will forgive many things but they do not forgive lack of preparation.

As part of your preparation, consider the needs of your audience. Why have they selected you to speak? What knowledge and experience do you have that will help them? Ultimately, what do these people need from you?

Once you have answered these questions, you can begin to tailor your remarks to suit their needs. Make the material your own by infusing your experiences and personality into the presentation. Your audience is your customer, and you should treat them like gold.

As part of your preparation, just like football, you need to practice. Rehearse your speech until it is second nature. Consistent with our "46 Attack Mindset," excuses will not be tolerated. There is no room for, "I didn't have enough time" or "My speechwriter didn't do what I wanted." Once again, we are responsible for all outcomes of our communication. It's always on us.

———

Here are several items to consider when preparing a speech or presentation:

a.) Who is your audience? What do they need from you? Are they potentially friendly or hostile?

b.) How long will you have to speak? Are you speaking before or after someone else? If so, what are the implications of that?

c.) What is the intention of your speech? Are you looking to:
   1. Educate?
   2. Inspire?
   3. Entertain?
It's always best if you can include aspects of all three.

d.) In one sentence, what is the central theme of your speech? As an example, if we were to provide a speaking theme for this book, it would be: *"We will teach you how to reach the upper limits of your genetic potential by learning how to control your mind and suppress your survival instincts."*

e.) What kind of interesting opening story might you lead with? How can you grab them from the outset?

f.) Consider telling your audience in your opening that you want them to leave with three major takeaways or ideas. Then tell them what they are.

g.) At the close of your speech, reiterate the three takeaways to ensure they've got it. Invite them to take immediate action.

Let's consider the second quality of a great speaker.

2) Be Comfortable – In order to make your audience comfortable, you will need to be relaxed and at ease. Your ability to appear comfortable gives you instant credibility.

    To make both the audience and yourself comfortable, there's a trick that some speakers use that often works. They pretend that they are the host of a party at their house. They act as if the audience is in their living room and they are simply there to make their guests feel at ease.

    This trick can be even more effective if there are opportunities to meet some of the audience before you take the stage. If you are out amongst them, you can ask them how they're doing and if they're comfortable. This preliminary contact humanizes you and can get people rooting for you before you even begin.

    Certainly, because you are only human, you may slip up and make a mistake. Or the technology may fail. Sometimes microphones and big screen visuals malfunction. If any of these things happen, remember that the number one key to success is how you handle adversity. Don't overreact and don't get emotional. Simply smile and laugh it off. Lighten up and use your sense of humor. Have a couple of "go-to" funny lines in your back pocket for when things go wrong.

    Finally, never show panic or fear. Simply carry on in the interests of serving everyone else in the room. If you can remember that it's not about you; it's about your audience, the customer – you can make the best of any situation.

3) Be Committed – The third quality of being a great speaker concerns the level of your commitment. Do you wholeheartedly believe what you're saying? The "46 Attack Mindset" demands that you are 100 percent all in on your topic.

    Being 100% committed to what you're saying takes care of things like vocal quality, body language and facial expression. When you are completely lit up and on fire about your subject matter, people feel your level of care. Your passion will bring the listener's level of interest up and your chances of educating, inspiring and entertaining your audience will rise exponentially.

Using eye contact is also crucial to connect with your audience. Proper eye contact is really akin to bringing your "A" game in the realm of communication. Ordinary communicators become extraordinary when they infuse eye contact along with the right attitude and an aggressive approach to their message. When you add in accountability to those you are speaking to, you cannot help but accomplish your communication goals.

4) Be Compelling – What does it mean to be compelling? It means to be anything but boring. The "46 Attack Mindset" advocates living to your maximum potential and that, by definition, means taking some risks. It means putting yourself out in front of people and sharing your knowledge and expertise.

Much like being prepared, no audience will forgive you for being uninteresting. Being compelling and committed go hand in hand.

In the past, corporate America taught leaders to be conservative when addressing their employees. No one was ever fired from corporate America for being boring. But times have changed. People expect you to be like the best speakers they see on television; interesting, animated and comfortable. Given two leaders of equal talent and ability, the one who can influence people and move them to action will be the one promoted.

In football, we used video to improve our performance. Seeing ourselves helped us to eliminate mistakes and improve our performance. It's the same with public speaking. Getting video of your performance provides terrific feedback. Once you see how you come across to others, you can make the necessary corrections.

Certainly, some people are more extroverted and it's easier for them to be animated. But that's not the only way to become more compelling. One of the easiest ways to become more compelling is to read outside of your field. No one has to be a one-trick pony. Knowing more about the world around you and being able to converse on many topics makes you a more interesting person.

Remember, public speaking is not a survival situation. If you find your mind treating it as such, once again, take a deep breath and seize control of your thought process. Remind yourself that you are well prepared and move beyond fear by focusing on the thing that needs to be done in the present moment.

If you are prepared, committed, comfortable and compelling, you will find yourself in the top 95th percentile of American speakers. Commit to improving in these areas and your successes will begin to compound.

The Power of Recognition and Reward

One of the most powerful communication tools at our disposal involves our ability to recognize and reward others. Nowhere was this more evident to me than during my time in the NFL.

Picture grown men making seriously good money playing professional football on a Sunday afternoon.

Were they thinking about the fact that they were on national television?

No.

Were they looking at the score?

No.

Were they thinking about making the playoffs?

No.

They were consumed to the point of obsession with winning the prize for the biggest hit in the game... *The Igloo Cooler.*

Winning the Igloo Cooler for the biggest hit meant that you would be recognized by your coaches and peers during the game film review on Monday. For those few moments, you were the dominant alpha male in a room full of testosterone-fueled achievers.

Now, the Igloo Cooler was a fine prize but it probably cost about $15. Any of us could have bought one without giving it a second thought. But the symbol of winning that award had us talking about it even during the games. I can remember one of our linebackers getting up after a hard hit declaring, "I think I just won the cooler!"

In hindsight, it's hilarious but it points out the power of recognition and reward, particularly among your peers. I've enjoyed watching current college teams like the University of Miami and the University of Georgia implement similar recognition awards during actual games. Miami rewards players who create turnovers with the "Turnover Chain." This massive gold chain is worn on the sideline by the player who comes up with a turnover until he once again takes the field. In a similar fashion, Georgia has implemented "Spiked Shoulder Pads" also worn by the player who takes the ball away.

These reward systems are taking hold with football teams across the country. Because people love recognition, I've used similar incentives in restaurants that I've owned. We would acknowledge and cheer great performances and even hand out grades to evaluate employees.

Whenever possible, we would align our employee recognition to being great with customers and thinking like an owner. When your employees begin thinking about greater service and cutting costs, you're doing something right.

It was also very important to listen to employee suggestions for improvement and constantly adapt and change to provide better service. My first year at Burger King, we were struggling to serve customers quickly at the drive-thru window. One of my employees recommended placing an employee with a wireless headset outside in the drive-thru lane near the menu board. They could go right to the customers' cars, expedite orders and collect the money.

This suggestion cut the drive-thru time in half. It also made a positive impact on the attitudes of our staff inside the restaurant. Maintaining that positive attitude can make or break a team. We worked to build our own "attitude team" within the restaurant. These were people we could trust, depend on and share our values with. Building your own "attitude team" is something you can do in your own business as well as your personal life.

Whatever we could do to reward both customers and employees was a win for the business. When it made sense, we would honor customer ideas with input they would give us in our suggestion boxes.

When looking at ways to reward employees, it often pays to think out of the box. In the world of fast food, it's common to have a high turnover rate with employees. Many of them are young people who lack stability in their lives. Others are heading off to college and for many, it's a first job. I realized I could save vast amounts of money if I could cut down on employee turnover. The cost of constantly training new people is very high. In addition, the mistakes that new employees make can also be costly.

Once again, being aggressive, I decided to try a uniquely different reward system.

It was always standard that employees could eat for free during their shifts. I took a risk and expanded that policy. I wanted to get the families of employees to have a stake in their children's employment. I began a policy that allowed immediate family members to come in any time and get any sandwich, a drink and fries for free. It was a radical notion at the time, but it saved money in the long term.

Here's an example of how it worked. I once had to let an employee go because he had failed to show up for a couple of his shifts. He was a fairly solid employee, but we had to maintain certain standards. The next thing I knew, he came in with his father to ask for his job back. As I had suspected, the family needed and appreciated that free food. It was important to them that their son keep his job. This kind of family investment and participation dramatically cut down on our training costs as people worked harder to keep their job.

In essence, it exhibited the same kind of family peer pressure that Buddy Ryan had created on our defense. This policy also contributed to a sense of team and community. Employees who stayed in their jobs got to know one another more closely. They also knew each other's strengths and weaknesses which made our food delivery systems flow more smoothly.

In both business and personal life, appropriately applied recognition and reward systems can dramatically improve everyone's experience of life. If you can create a happy atmosphere where people want to come to work and be productive, your chances of success will explode. Teams and workers often take on the personalities of their coaches and managers. You can set the tone of your team's personality by your own behavior and attitude.

Can you imagine your success if everyone on your team came in with the "46 Attack Mindset?" *What would happen if everyone came in with their "A" game every single day?*

That's your challenge as a leader. You can teach these principles every day. You can cover one aspect of everyone's "A" game in the morning huddle. You can reward the person who exhibits the best attitude or aggressively makes the most changes to improve your business. You can make the "46 Attack Mindset" an integral part of your operating system.

Even if you're not the leader, you can still set the example. Be the one who comes in with their "A" game. Be the one who comes in and listens to others. Be the first, the fastest and the best in everything you do.

Be the one who recognizes the boss! Bosses are people too. They have headaches and problems and are generally working very hard on your behalf. Thank them. Write them a note. Remember their birthday. *You will not believe the difference this can make!* No matter who you are or what your position is within an organization, you can turn the entire atmosphere around if you take this on. Plus, it's fun!

Learn about what motivates each person. When I was a head coach in the Arena League, I got to know all of my players on a personal level. This gave me a sense of how I could best motivate each one. Everyone is different. If you can learn about what drives each individual, you can tailor your reward structure accordingly.

Most importantly, continue to give serious thought to how you recognize and reward others. If you can keep an open mind towards how you might reward business partners, colleagues, and friends, you might just find yourself the biggest winner in your own game of life.

———

Fire Fast, Hire Slow

As someone who has run teams and organizations, I'm often asked about communicating personnel decisions. I believe in the philosophy of "fire fast, hire slow."

The longer you wait to get rid of the nonperformers, the more damage you do to your organization. Certainly, give them a chance to succeed. Coach them up. Give them a probationary period. None of us have known everything about a job when we first began. For example, when I told the Bears that I had extensive experience playing safety, I knew I had to learn quickly because I had in fact, never played the position.

But they gave me a chance and I made them glad that they did.

Not everyone is able to succeed in that fashion. In most jobs, you can tell fairly quickly who's going to produce positive results and who won't. It's often just a matter of reading their attitude. If a person's attitude is bad, it won't matter if they're a genius. No one is going to want to work with them.

But everyone occasionally needs advice and direction. This is true in both business and sports. I have found many similarities between the two. If a player or an employee is doing something wrong, it must be addressed and corrected immediately. By allowing a behavior to continue, it sends a message to others that management or the coaching staff does not care. Or it suggests that they have preferences for certain people.

Employees and players begin to feel that "If they can do it, then I can do it." The overall situation deteriorates because the situation is not being handled and confidence in the leadership begins to erode.

When I was a football coach, there was a slogan that totally captured this concept.

"You are either endorsing it or are allowing it to happen."

I found that as a coach and business man, if I did not correct a situation quickly, it came back to bite me at a crucial moment in either a game or a business situation.

One of the methods I used to correct behaviors was called a "criticism sandwich."

It's common in sports for a coach to immediately scream at a player when he wants to correct that player's actions or behavior. Obviously, that won't typically work in a business situation, particularly in today's environment.

Whether as a football coach or a business owner, I found the most effective way of making a correction was to speak privately with the individual. And it was important to do it as soon as I became aware of the improper behavior.

I began by finding something positive about the person. I would get their attention and give them a compliment to start the conversation. I would then quickly move to the action that needed to be corrected. That portion of the conversation would require the most time and attention.

After detailing the mistake, I would provide the correct alternative action by telling them how, showing them how, and then allowing them to do it properly. This correction process was forceful, direct, and in detail. To conclude the conversation, I would leave them with a positive note about how much I appreciated their work ethic and personality. This "criticism sandwich" allowed both of us to walk away feeling good about ourselves because the criticism had been carefully placed between compliments.

After you've given your employees a fair chance to succeed, don't wait to remove those who are the weak links. Help them in any way that you can, but remember Mike Ditka's words at his first team meeting. He said, "Many of you will not be here next year."

Mike removed the nonperformers and was able to build a Super Bowl Championship Team.

Too often, we allow the weak links to "control the agenda." This means that, unlike Ditka, we make excuses for those who are late or we cover for those who don't have the competency to succeed at the task they've been given. Sometimes we just don't want to have that difficult conversation when we have to let them go.

While it may seem harsh to "fire fast" – it's actually the most compassionate thing to do. Your other employees should not have to cover for those who cannot perform. In addition, your customers and stockholders deserve to see the best team and talent working on their behalf. And the person that you're letting go can get started sooner on learning new skills and finding another job.

On the other hand, when hiring, I always recommend taking your time. Learn as much as you can about the person. What's their background? What's their record of success? What references do they have? How do they stack up on the six components of "A" game?

You can get a preliminary assessment of their "A" game simply by asking the following:

How's their attitude? Are they aggressive? Have they been able to anticipate and plan their life properly? How have they handled adversity? Who are they accountable to? And finally, what have they accomplished so far?

Simply by focusing on these "A" game components, you can learn just about everything you need to know.

Above all, take whatever time you need when hiring. If you make a mistake in hiring, you have to go back to the drawing board and fire, rehire, and retrain. Hiring properly will save you time and money in the long run.

———

Body Language

No section on communication would be complete without a few words about body language. While we alluded to it earlier when summarizing the 13 Elements of Control, it's worth revisiting in another context.

In the NFL, reading body language was a very important part of my game. In the defensive secondary, we constantly had to watch for receivers and backs going in motion and looking for "tells" that a quarterback might give to tip off a play. Most importantly, once the ball was snapped, we had to discern whether the play was a run or a pass.

The body language of the offensive linemen gave us the most information. Offensive linemen are not allowed to go downfield on a pass play. So if they immediately moved forward, the play was a run. When the linemen took a step back, they were pass blocking. I typically watched the offensive guards because they gave us the most information. Occasionally, they would "pull" to move out around the end to lead blocking for a run or a screen pass.

Watching the opposition's body language could also tell us a little bit about how tired they were or if they might be injured. We had to be careful with this though. Throughout history, there have been great running backs who would get up very slowly after being tackled. Not everyone bounced up like the great Walter Payton. Both Jim Brown and O.J. Simpson used to get up as if they were on their last legs. They would limp back to their huddle looking completely spent. You would have thought they were all but ready for the retirement home. But then they would explode on the next play. So, it paid to be a bit discerning in how we read body language.

———

Our body language and appearance are the first thing people judge when they see us. First impressions get formed within the first five to seven seconds of meeting us. Unless we do something dramatic to change that initial reaction, people will typically hold on to that first impression. For one thing, they don't like to change their opinion because they don't like to admit, even to themselves, that they were wrong.

For another thing, people will go to a lot of trouble to remain consistent in their viewpoints. Consistency in our values and beliefs is generally rewarded in this culture. People who appear inconsistent in their viewpoints are often called wishy-washy and indecisive. As such, people will go to great lengths to remain uniform in their opinions.

The lesson? Be intentional about the impression you want to create when you first meet someone. There's a good chance that whatever label they give you will stick.

In the NFL, if a guy came into the league and fumbled a couple times early in his career, he'd get labeled. *That guy's a fumbler*. Even if he went two years without a fumble after that, the label would often stay with him.

Other times, the label would become a self-fulfilling prophecy. I saw guys get labeled and they would believe whatever tag they were given. This could work either for or against them. If a guy got labeled as a fumbler and believed it, he'd continue to fumble. If another guy got labeled as a big hitter and he believed it, he became a big hitter. This is simply another facet of "see it, believe it and achieve it" that we discussed in our "A" game.

Being conscious of the initial impression we give to others can go a long way towards success. When we present the best version of ourselves, we often get treated as the best version of ourselves. Others will tend to believe whatever we project.

Here are just a few things to consider as we take charge of our body language and the initial impression we give to others.

1) How is my posture? Am I standing up straight?
2) Am I giving off a positive and friendly vibe? Do I have a pleasant demeanor with the appropriate level of enthusiasm?
3) Am I listening closely to what others are saying? Did I catch their name?
4) Am I absorbing what's going on in the surroundings? Different events harbor different moods.
5) Am I making others comfortable and adding value to the environment?

Once we've mastered the basics of our initial impression, we can look at how we can take our communication skills to the next level.

Chapter Four – Control the Environment:
Presence, Power and Warmth

Motivation is like a tire. You have to keep pumping it up!

Doug Plank

I can remember being a teenager and gaining confidence as an athlete. I was having success in both football and baseball. But I really didn't know how I would stack up against major competition beyond high school.

One day, the great George Blanda came to speak at a local football dinner I attended. George had been a star at Youngwood High School in Pennsylvania before going on to be an All-Conference quarterback and place kicker at the University of Kentucky. At Kentucky, he was coached by the legendary Paul "Bear" Bryant before Bryant went to Alabama. After college, George went on to have a storied career in professional football. Over a 26-year pro career, George played for the Chicago Bears, Houston Oilers and Oakland Raiders before retiring at the age of 48.

Meeting George was a pivotal experience for me. He was a shade under six feet two and muscular with an impressive handshake. But he was not enormous and I was encouraged to see that he was not that much bigger than me. We were practically eye to eye.

George had what we commonly call charisma. In listening to him, I became incredibly motivated. I came to believe that I could compete beyond high school football. George gave me a sense of my own possibility. If he could do it, I could do it. His influence gave me hope and belief that I carried forward through high school and beyond.

When was the last time you helped someone see their own potential through your eyes?

People don't lack potential or capability. They only lack someone to hold the mirror up to them and tell them of their own greatness. This is motivation at its best.

Most people are very hard on themselves. If just one person steps up and reminds them of their own strengths, it can turn them completely around. It can give them the impetus to go on and do powerful things.

That's what meeting George Blanda did for me. He allowed me to see that perhaps I too, could excel at the highest levels of athletics.

Charisma

We often hear the word charisma bandied about as an essential quality of an effective communicator. It may or may not be essential, but in a world where media is ever-present, it's a useful influence tool. And those who have it are outstanding motivators.

What is charisma?

People who have charisma are comfortable in their own skin. They bring a certain energy with them that allows them to control the atmosphere in a room. They usually cause others to react to them more than they react to others.

Charismatic people are generally mission-driven. They are purposeful and clear on their values and beliefs. More often than not, they exude three qualities that authors such as Amy Cuddy and Olivia Fox Cabane have outlined in their studies.

Those qualities are 1) presence, 2) power and 3) warmth.

Presence

When you are present with someone, you focus all of your mental and emotional energy on them. You make them feel as if they are the most important person in the world. The best way to accomplish this is to ask them questions. People love to talk about themselves. Yet how many times have you gone out to dinner and watched people at their tables giving all of their attention to their cell phone? Or have you watched people at a bus stop, or at a gym or even walking down the street? Their heads are down buried in the cyber world.

With all of the distractions common in our world today, it's easy to lose our presence. But even in our changing technological times, people still want to be recognized and acknowledged. Otherwise, Facebook, Instagram, Twitter and other cyber-connectivity avenues wouldn't be so popular.

I sometimes think of that old song written by Stephen Stills, "Love the One You're With." Giving all of your attention to the person in front of you is a great gift. Think of the influence advantage you can have if you simply put your cell phone down and listen intently to that person. Practice bringing yourself into the here and now. Stop thinking about yesterday and tomorrow. Look the person in the eyes and make them the momentary center of the universe. Not only do you avoid misunderstanding but you show deep respect and care to that person.

If you focus intently on the person in front of you, your charisma factor will rise exponentially.

Power

Power is the second factor within the Charisma triad. People who practice the "46 Attack Mindset" typically already have this one covered. Why? Because they get things accomplished. People who get things done have already begun to work their way up the power curve.

Powerful people tend to have resources and status. This creates a primal attraction because humans are drawn to wealth and authority. But sometimes being powerful simply means that you influence and impact the world around you. This again gets back to our "get off first" aggressive approach to everything we do. You will often build a following simply by being the "unreasonable" one who takes the risk or brings the first good idea to the table. Power, courage and risk go hand in hand.

If you are consistently bringing your "A" game and practicing the 13 Elements of Control we outlined earlier, you will already be well on the way to mastering the power component of charisma. Your competence will show through.

Remember that your confidence and carriage can project an extremely powerful presence. If you back that up with accomplishment, you only need to consider one more factor in your charisma triad…

Warmth

With presence and power, you can seem imposing and important, but without warmth, you will not have the kind of influential charisma that truly motivates people to move mountains.

Warmth is the factor that will keep you from being perceived as arrogant, distant, and unapproachable. You might be able to get away with being a jerk for a while, but eventually it will come back to haunt you.

Genuine warmth, combined with power and presence, can rally people to great causes. I use the word genuine because warmth is difficult to fake. People can usually tell if you want something from them.

Authentic and real warmth comes from a service-oriented mindset that begins with a good heart. People who project warmth are curious about others and have empathy for their situations. They typically practice gratitude and treat others with the kind of respect they wish to receive.

Practicing warmth can be as simple as making people feel comfortable. Relax, smile and be kind. It's often as easy as that.

Charisma, like all communication skills, is something that can be developed with work and practice. Reaching the upper limits of our genetic potential in communication is something that we can practice until our very last breath. We can always improve.

Communication is a part of our "46 Attack Mindset" because it pervades every aspect of our lives. And its presence will be felt in this book's final challenge to you.

Life is a journey, a process. Much of it is out of your control. The "46 Attack Mindset" has centered on taking charge of your mind and the things that *are* in your control. As we close, we introduce another concept that many might find unreasonable. I am challenging you – and me – to make the last thing we ever do the greatest thing we ever do.

SECTION THREE: Making the Last Thing You Ever Do Your Greatest

Chapter Five – Attack to the Very End

I will never voluntarily go into glide path mode. I am fascinated by the idea of making the last thing I ever do – the greatest thing I ever do.

Doug Plank

Life is a game.

It has a beginning and an end. Within this game there are players, coaches and owners. In the beginning, everyone is a player. From there, some move up to become coaches and a few even become owners.

But no matter who you become, there is a beginning and an end. No one gets out of this game alive.

Unlike in sports, we do not have the benefit of a clock. There are no innings to keep track of where you are. There is no scoreboard to tell you if you are ahead or behind.

Without notification or warning, the game could end at any time.

Recognizing this, each day I wonder what I could do that I've never done before. What effort could I exert today that would leave a lasting memory after I die?

Legacy

I'm fascinated by the idea of legacy. Legacy is a major part of life yet no one teaches us about it. I'm aware of no class in how to create your legacy.

In reality, your legacy might be something as simple as how you go about your daily life. Or it might involve a major task that requires others to help. But whatever it is, give some thought to what you leave behind. Give some thought to how you want to be remembered.

Apart from just material things, I hope to be remembered for 100% effort and how I worked to get the most out of my mind and body. Even more, I want to be remembered as the guy who worked to make challenges fun and meaningful.

One of my favorite memories of facing a challenge occurred during my time at Ohio State. During the summer months, we could either go home, work, or continue to take classes. I decided to stay in Columbus and work at the Anheuser Busch brewery along with some of the other Ohio State football players. We would normally work twelve hour shifts in order to get overtime in the draft beer section. It was pretty good money and most of us needed it.

The work challenged us because it was extremely physical. It required that we lift beer kegs and place them on an assembly line before cleaning, sterilizing and removing the wooden cork. It was tough, but it was perfect summer work for football players who actually had the strength to perform the labor.

Like any good company wanting to improve, the Anheuser Busch Company kept records of how many kegs were prepared for filling on each shift. So, I began to wonder just how difficult it would be to prepare more kegs than any other shift had previously readied. After all, as an athlete, I enjoyed competition. I thought back to those days working on my uncle's garbage trucks and how we had turned the work into a game. If you could make work into a game, time passed more quickly, the challenge became more fun, and everyone came out ahead.

So, one day I was working with the other football players. I said, "Let's show these people what you can get done with a little effort. Let's see how fast we can do this. Let's set a new record."

It didn't take long. Within the first three days of working with these other competitive athletes, we were crushing previous records. The workers on the assembly line were begging us to slow down. We were going so fast that we were overloading the system with clean, sterilized beer kegs and the other assembly line workers could not keep up with our level of production.

For us, the competitive athletes, it didn't seem like work because we had turned the process of cleaning draft beer kegs into a competitive game. We were no longer just workers. We were a record-setting team.

What if you could turn all of life into a game?

What if you could make your day-to-day challenges fun and bring a spirit of excellence and high quality to every trial you face?

That might turn out to be your legacy!

You might be the person remembered as the one who brought positive energy and a fun, competitive spirit to every task.

Think about how you might be able to transform your work environment with that kind of attitude.

Think about how you might inject that kind of enthusiasm within your family and friends.

Whatever you do, I encourage you to think about your legacy.

I once heard it said that you die twice. The first time you die is in reality.

The second time you die is the last time anyone utters your name.

You can begin to build your legacy right now. How do you want to be remembered?

———

Somewhere along the way, humans invented the idea of retirement. Personally, I don't believe that retirement is a natural phenomenon. Before the concept of retirement was conceived, humans contributed all the way up until their death. Wisdom was valued and passed along. Resources collected over a lifetime were shared.

The "46 Attack Mindset" does not recognize retirement. There is no place for planned obsolescence in this philosophy. People are not disposable products. They are not designed to be put out to pasture. As long as I have a single pulse left in my body, I want to stay in the game and contribute in whatever way I can.

Certainly, we all face challenges as we get older. But those of us who choose to be unreasonable work to make our capabilities exceed our limitations. We always set a high bar. Why wouldn't we?

On the football field, I wanted to expend every drop of sweat and effort that I had. I didn't want to leave anything on the playing field.

It's the same in life. I don't want to waste all of the lessons I've learned. I want to use and share my knowledge. I want to know that at the end of the day, I gave every ounce of myself to teach, help, train and empower people of all ages.

I particularly want to assist those who want to serve. Whether you are fifteen years old or ninety, I want you to use the "46 Attack Mindset" to tackle the day and be the best you can be.

For me, retirement is simply a frame of mind. It has nothing to do with whether you go to an office or draw a paycheck. As long as you are learning, growing and doing your best to add value to whatever circumstances you are in, you are not retired.

———

We've been taught and "mentally programmed" by the culture to give in when we get older. If we have a few aches and pains we're supposed to give up. We are encouraged to let everyone else live fulfilling lives while we watch.

No.

Once again, swimming against the current and being unreasonable, we can look at this differently. *The aches and pains that we have are directly proportional to the amount of wisdom and experience we can share.*

If you don't hurt somewhere, you probably haven't lived.

I'm not suggesting you enjoy the hurt, but I do suggest that you respect it. It generally means that you've been through experiences that you and others can draw from. It's time to leverage that experience. But you have to be willing to acknowledge and share what you've experienced in some form or fashion.

It might be that you share it in writing. It might be that you speak in public. It might be that you have intimate conversations in coffee shops. It might be that you share your experience with your kids or grandkids. Maybe you volunteer in elementary schools. Whatever and wherever it is, your experience is valuable to someone.

Own it.

Use it.

Share it.

Sharing your experience may not be entirely comfortable. But growing through the discomfort is the point. That's where your continued growth lies as you advance in years.

Whenever I begin to get uncomfortable through fatigue or frustration, I think of Winston Churchill's iconic words. He said:

"The pessimist sees the problems in every opportunity. Whereas the optimist sees opportunity in every problem."

Even more importantly, Churchill said:

> "Never give in, never give in, never; never, never, never – in nothing, great or small, large or petty – never give in except to convictions of honor and good sense."

Like Churchill, you can harden yourself to never stop and never quit. My experiences in football and as a business owner have hardened and toughened me, while also making me more compassionate with people who struggle through circumstances that they cannot control.

So how do you keep your perseverance muscle strong when that quitting conversation begins to take hold in your mind?

You get back to what you stand for and you keep that edge that's always served you through the tough times.

No matter how old you are, you never need to lose your edge.

When I played football, my edge was my attitude. I showed up with bad intentions. But those bad intentions allowed me to perform at my highest level in order to help my team accomplish its good intentions.

In order to keep my edge, *I took a stand.*

My stand was that I would never let my teammates, my brothers down.

My stand was that I was going to get the most out of my body and my mind.

No matter how much pain I was in; no matter what kind of injuries I'd incurred; I was going to show up for the team. I was going to give 100%. NO MATTER WHAT!

They were going to have to carry me out on a stretcher before I would give up.

That's how I'd been trained at Ohio State and that's what sustained me in the NFL. I've done my best to keep that attitude and that edge as I've gone forward throughout my life.

Keeping my edge was never about how much money I made. It was never about the clothes I wore or the kind of car I drove.

It was about how I showed up for the team when they needed me most.

Since my playing days, it's been about how I show up for my family, friends and business associates when they need me most.

As people, we all struggle with similar challenges throughout our lives. We struggle with jobs and relationships. We have family and friends who get sick and eventually die. We also have illnesses and injuries to handle until our time is up.

Given this, how do we keep our edge?

How do we work towards making the last thing we do our greatest?

First, we define what we stand for.

Second, we simply go back to the question we asked in chapter one.

"What am I going to get done?"

This sometimes requires that we forget about how we feel and just get back to what we need to do.

Take a Stand and Design Your Character

We've already discovered that life is a game. Within this game, there is opportunity.

From wherever you are, you can design yourself. You have the ability to create your intentions and design your own character. This is a gift that the universe has given each of us. Yet many people never even consider designing their character.

The word reinvention gets thrown around a lot. If that idea has appeal, you can reinvent yourself. You can define just what you stand for and what your character and behavior will be going forward.

But just what is character?

Character is sometimes defined as the mental and moral qualities distinctive to an individual. I believe that character is revealed by who you are when no one is looking.

Are you consistently acting with discipline?

Are you acting with integrity and doing what you committed to?

Are you doing the right thing?

Character is about behavior. It's much more important than "talk."

While talent is a gift, character is a choice. When you are of good character, your relationships improve because people can trust you. When you think of the greatest leaders in history, these were almost always people of great character. You may not always agree with them; you may not even like them, but you could trust them to do what they said they were going to do.

In the past, leaders like George Halas, Vince Lombardi, Abraham Lincoln and Winston Churchill were nothing if not consistent in their words and deeds. You knew where they stood so you never had to guess what kinds of behaviors would be rewarded or punished.

It's even more imperative in today's world that successful leaders create relationships built on integrity and trust. With the ascent of social media, it's very easy to get caught saying one thing but doing another. Certainly no one is perfect. But too often, we see people's character revealed through a tweet or a text that harms themselves and the people they're supposed to be leading.

Successful leaders in today's world give people hope. Similar to that "criticism sandwich" that we spoke of earlier, we want to leave people feeling good about themselves and their potential. When we send them off expecting their best, we give them something to live up to.

Great leaders also generously share themselves and their knowledge. Withholding useful information helps no one. We need to give our people the knowledge and benefit of our successes and failures. Teddy Roosevelt said that, "He who makes no mistakes makes no progress. But the team that keeps making the same mistakes also makes no progress." Therefore, it's critical that we give everything that we can of ourselves to help others succeed.

How? Once again, we tell people how to succeed. Then we show them how to succeed. Finally, we step back and allow them to succeed. I stress this throughout the book because giving proper direction to your team or your staff is often the simple difference between success and failure.

It's also essential that your team see you continuing to improve and work on yourself. Being of good character, it is incumbent upon you to commit to furthering your own education and knowledge. You will set a terrific example for your team if you personally commit to continuous improvement.

No matter your age, you can improve your character and rewrite your own story beginning right now. You can begin anew.

This is significant because inherent in our *"What am I going to get done?"* question is an important concept. The very question itself drives us to the concept of creation.

We currently have a society based on consumption. We are a nation of consumers. There's nothing intrinsically wrong with consumption. *But to keep your edge, you need to be a creator.*

We need more creators. It's the creators that drive the economy and produce jobs. It's the creators that take responsibility for the kind of society they want to live in. It's the creators who are too busy producing content and products to be wrapped up in television, pop culture and things that keep us busy as opposed to productive.

Certainly, everyone enjoys television, movies, sports, music and the arts. I love watching a great sporting event and I enjoy doing color commentary on football games. We all value entertainment. The problem occurs when we allow consuming these products to take over all of our free time when in fact, *we could be starring in our own lives.*

If you haven't been starring in your own life, you can begin today. And by starring in your own life, I don't mean being a self-obsessed, me-first personality. I'm simply talking about engaging with your own possibilities.

So much of life is simply there for you to *take.*

You don't get life back and you don't get to go backwards. You can't turn back the clock. But you don't need to. Remember, it's not how you start, it's how you finish! You can control how you go forward. And as the "46 Attack Mindset" suggests, you can bring all of your energy to your present moment and seize every opportunity in front of you.

What? You don't see an opportunity?

If no opportunity exists, get proactive. Get aggressive. Remember who you are! You're on my team now. You are embracing the "46 Attack Mindset" and you can *create your own opportunity!*

Now I can almost hear some of you saying, "But Doug! I have limitations that I didn't have when I was younger. I'm not as capable as I once was."

Believe me, I understand. I get that. Like I mentioned earlier, life accumulates. Some of that accumulation doesn't always favor us.

But this is where the "46 Attack Mindset" teaches us that *we must work to make our capabilities exceed our limitations!*

Make Your Capabilities Exceed Your Limitations

During my entire football career, I played with injuries. Knees, ribs, shoulders, concussions, you name it, I played with it. Practically everyone in the NFL, past or present, has dealt with these same challenges.

Injuries limited us, often in big ways. But we had to find a way to keep playing hard and at the highest level, regardless of our physical impairments. For me, that sometimes meant leading with my head.

If my shoulders and ribs were incapacitated, I would throw myself into a tackle head first. This "spearing" technique of tackling is no longer legal but at the time, it was the way that I could compensate for my injuries – and it was effective. It was a way of making my capabilities exceed my limitations.

But that is a fairly extreme example. It's difficult for the average person to be able to relate to that. So I sometimes use the following example that is a bit more relatable to people who have not played professional football.

Back in the 1960's and 70's, the late writer and Hollywood columnist, Joe Hyams, was very much into martial arts. As such, he used to write best-selling biographies for people like Chuck Norris. At one time, Joe was taking martial arts lessons from the great Bruce Lee. This was at a time when Bruce was trying to get himself established in Hollywood as an actor. To make money, he was teaching self-defense to a number of celebrities.

As Joe approached his 50th birthday, he began complaining. He was telling Bruce that he felt he was getting too old to really achieve much more with Jeet-Kune-Do, the martial art that Bruce created and taught.

Bruce would have none of it. Bruce explained that people can never learn anything new until they are ready to accept themselves *with* their limitations. He explained that Joe would need to accept the fact that he was capable in some areas while limited in others. The challenge, he explained, was that Joe needed to further develop the capabilities that he still had.

Joe wasn't convinced. He continued to complain by saying that ten years ago, he could easily kick over his head. But now it took him 30 minutes just to limber up enough to do it.

Bruce said, "That was ten years ago. So, you are older today and your body has changed. Everyone has physical limitations to overcome."

Joe countered, "Well that's easy for you to say! If ever a man was born with natural ability to be a martial artist, it is you."

Bruce laughed at him and said, "I'm going to tell you something very few people know. I became a martial artist in spite of my limitations. My right leg is an inch shorter than the left. That is why I stand with my left foot leading. Then I found that because my right leg was shorter, I had an advantage with certain kinds of kicks, since the uneven stomp gave me greater impetus."

He continued, "And I wear contact lenses. I have been near-sighted since childhood, which has meant that if I wasn't wearing glasses, I couldn't see opponents unless they were up close. I had to create an ideal fighting technique for up close – *to make my capabilities exceed my limitations*. I accepted my limitations for what they were and capitalized on them. And that's what you must learn to do!"

Bruce let that sink in before he went on. "You say you are unable to kick over your head without a long warm-up, but the real question is, is it really necessary to kick that high? The fact is, until recently, martial artists rarely kicked above knee height. Head-high kicks are mostly for show. So perfect your kicks at waist level and below and they will be so formidable that you will never need to kick higher."

Bruce continued, "Instead of trying to do everything well, do those things perfectly of which you are capable."

Joe came back with, "But the fact still remains that my real competition is the advancing years."

Bruce said, "Stop comparing yourself with the person you were twenty years ago. The past is an illusion. You must learn to live in the present and accept yourself for who and where you are now. What you lack in flexibility and agility you must make up for with knowledge and practice."*

As we know, Bruce definitely practiced what he preached because he became an international movie star against all odds. If we discover our strong points, we can work to make them outweigh our weaknesses.

*Hyams, Joe. *Zen in the Martial Arts*. Bantam, 1982.

I love that example because all of us at some point feel the physical effects of age.

So, the questions become, "What are the limitations I am currently dealing with?"

And, "What is still available to me?"

How might all of us make our capabilities exceed our limitations?

———

As we look at making the last thing we ever do our greatest, some self-reflection is in order. As part of this reflection, I'm going to pose a question that you've probably never been asked.

What's your superpower?

I've had some people tell me that my energy and my ability to get the most out of my mind and body is my superpower. I appreciate that thought and I hope that it's true.

But when asked, I've always believed that with some effort, I could positively change the energy of any room I walked into. That's a power that I've tried to use to create upbeat and constructive environments. Whether as a coach of a team, or as an owner of a business, creating a winning environment is a power I've always tried to cultivate.

I believe that we can all cultivate the superpower of *influence.*

While owning restaurants, I would occasionally see someone who might look like they were having a bad day. I would silently challenge myself to see if I could somehow make them smile. Maybe I could even make their day. It was really satisfying if I could turn their mood around and make them laugh. It was a win for everyone.

We had one regular customer who was very curmudgeonly. He never smiled. Never. You've probably known people like this. Finally, I couldn't take it. We all knew him by name so I went up to him and said, "Ralph, you're a great customer. We really appreciate that you come in every day. I want you to try some of these new dessert options we're testing out. On the house."

He eyed me somewhat suspiciously but said, "Okay."

I then brought an entire tray of every dessert we had to his table. It could have fed a third world country.

I said, "Enjoy, Ralph – and let me know which ones you like the best."

Nothing. No smile. He just kind of nodded.

Walking back to the counter, under my breath I said, "Wow, this is one nut that may be just too tough to crack."

As we all continued to work, I watched Ralph calmly and deliberately consume the desserts out of the corner of my eye.

He seemed to be enjoying himself but I had pretty much given up the idea that we were going to get a reaction from him. He finished and we all were caught off guard as he slowly walked up to the counter.

He said with just a hint of a grin, "Thanks. That was good."

Victory.

I think the entire staff and I felt like we'd just kicked a game-ending, fifty-four-yard field goal to win the Super Bowl.

The significance of this story is simply that you never know the impact you can have. Ralph continued to come in and while he didn't have a complete personality overhaul, he exhibited a warmth that hadn't been there before. He now knew that there was a place where he could go where he was recognized, valued and appreciated.

We all have this power of influence to lift people up. Similar to the letter that I wrote to Arthur Blank, the smallest kindness or gesture can have a huge ripple effect. Each of us has power that we don't even realize.

One of the first times I realized the power of my own influence came early in my career with the Bears. I was asked by a position coach to go and talk to a young high school football player after the season. The young man was a fan of mine and lived in Pittsburgh, close to where I grew up.

When I arrived at his home, I was surprised to see that he was in a wheelchair sitting in the living room. During the football season he had suffered several cracked vertebrae in the lower region of his spine. He had movement in his arms but not his legs.

After an hour of conversation, he said he would like to show me something in his bedroom. He directed me into his bedroom and he showed me a few trophies and footballs. He unexpectedly pointed to the ceiling above his bed. Upon closer inspection, it was a picture of a Chicago Bear player making a tackle and I could barely make out the word Plank on the back of the jersey.

He said, "Mr. Plank, you are the first person I see in the morning and last person I see at night. You motivate me to keep going when I want to quit."

I swallowed hard.

At that moment, it really dawned on me that as a professional athlete, I had influence beyond my own understanding. I realized that I had the potential to influence others without even knowing it. And at the risk of sounding cliché, I resolved to myself at that moment that I would begin to use that power for good.

Over time, I also understood that influence and affluence don't always go hand in hand. There are many people who are rich and famous but they don't necessarily use the influence they have in a positive way.

My time with that young athlete taught me that I could make a difference.

In life, we do not make this journey alone. There have only been a couple of people that have ever climbed Mt. Everest by themselves. I encourage you to recognize the influence that you have. Like me with that young man, you may not even be aware of it. Sometimes we think our children don't hear what we say or see what we do. Years later, we realize that they heard and saw everything.

You have influence over every person you come into contact with. It could be at work. It could be at the gym. It could be at the grocery store.

Influence is neutral until you use it. It is similar to money. It can be used for good or bad. You could save it and never use it. Or you could attempt to change the world beginning with the person in front of you.

That's the decision I made when I met that young football player.

Each of us has the power to change lives. But we must recognize it, exercise it, and maximize it.

Innovation

Perhaps your superpower revolves around innovation. It could be that you are the person that always comes up with a new and better way of doing things.

This is truly a superpower and it takes us back to that idea of creation. Instead of just following the herd and doing things the way they've always been done, you are the person who takes the risk of trying a new way.

When I coached in the Arena League, I was always looking for ways to innovate. Anything that could gain us a competitive advantage was worth looking at.

I've always said, "Rulebooks are made to be read." Yet hardly anyone ever reads them.

I studiously poured over the Arena League rules in an effort to exploit them to our advantage. I could always find a few gray areas where what you could or could not do wasn't made clear in the rulebook. As such, I forced a couple of rule changes during my time with the league.

Similar to Canadian football, in the Arena League, receivers can move forward towards the line of scrimmage before the ball is snapped. This gives offenses a great advantage because the momentum of the receiver's head start makes it very difficult for defensive backs to cover them.

To counter this, instead of having my defenders backpedaling to try and keep up with the receivers, I would have them come forward and aggressively hit the receivers at the line of scrimmage. This was completely in keeping with the "46 Attack Mindset."

It was similar to the old "bump and run" idea but much more aggressive. The receivers were quite shocked to be bludgeoned as they were building their momentum. One day, during a nationally televised Arena League game, the league commissioner communicated his displeasure with this defensive tactic to our bench. We were told that any further contact with the motion receiver would result in fines for our owner and suspension of the head coach.

Well, I certainly didn't want our owner fined and I didn't want to be suspended so that was the end of that particular strategy. But it reinforced to me that a mindset that attacks pays dividends.

Perhaps my most fun, and in retrospect, most humorous innovation was what we called "the burn package."

The Arena League is characterized by high scoring and it's essentially an offensive show. Almost every possession ends in some kind of score. Clock management becomes critical because if you have to give the ball back at the end of a close game, you will probably lose. The odds are always that the offense will score.

As a result, I came up with the burn package. This amounted to burning the clock down to zero at the end of a game. I would replace my offensive starters with my best tacklers. I would then replace my quarterback with my fastest and best athlete. As opposed to a traditional offensive block, at the snap of the ball I instructed my "blockers" to tackle the defender in front of them. I encouraged them to lay on top of them and hold them down for as long as they could. Whatever they needed to do to keep their man occupied was all fair game.

The quarterback, with the ball, would then run around the field for as long as he could. It was like a game of keep-away or tag. I would have him run to one end of the field and then to the other. The idea was to run the clock for as long as possible. Of course, we would be penalized ten yards for holding when they finally caught him, but it might take two minutes for that to happen –and boom – the game was over. We would have to run one more snap after the penalty where we would just take a knee and the game would end.

Well, as you might imagine, this didn't sit well with the league and yes, the burn package also became illegal.

I'm told that I'm the only coach in the history of professional football that ever got some kind of communication from a league commissioner during a game with instructions to change what we were doing. I don't know if that is true but I take it as a badge of honor because, after all, innovation is at the heart of creation.

Even when it becomes illegal.

———

If you think about it, there really are an infinite number of superpowers. You might be the person that doesn't care what others think. That means rejection doesn't bother you. That can be a superpower.

You might be the person that shares your abundance with others. That could be time, energy or money. Properly allocated, your sharing of your abundance is a superpower.

You might be the person that will donate organs in case of accidental or early death. That's a tremendous gift and as such, a superpower.

Whatever you define your superpower to be, use it. Embrace it.

Remember, you have influence.

––––

As we begin to wrap up our study of the "46 Attack Mindset" – and as we contemplate making the last thing we ever do our greatest – I want to briefly examine one more concept.

The power of the human spirit.

The awesome power of the human spirit is greater than any substance or temptation that you've ever confronted.

It is greater than any obstacle you face.

Your body may break down but your mind can always grow stronger. Your will can become unbreakable.

Your spirit can become indomitable.

Mark Twain once said, "Most men die at 27; we just bury them at 72."

It doesn't have to be that way.

Don't wait any longer. Don't put things off. Don't make excuses.

Always, always…stop thinking about what's going to happen to you and focus on what you need to get done.

––––

Not long ago, the power of my own human spirit was tested greatly. It was the middle of the night on February 17th, 2018. Driving from Denver to my home in Scottsdale, my truck hit a patch of ice. I wasn't speeding, but my truck didn't know that. In the blink of an eye, my truck and I were airborne. I held on for dear life. Upon landing, the truck began to bounce and roll; eight revolutions according to a motorist behind me.

For all of the crazy crashes I had initiated years before in the NFL, this one was something completely different – and unexpected. I literally had a death grip on the wheel. Thank God I had stopped to get gas a few minutes before and had put my seatbelt on. That wasn't always a given. I always wear my seatbelt now.

Once the truck stopped bouncing, I knew I was hurt badly. Bleeding profusely, my immediate focus was to somehow crawl out of the driver's side window. Later at the hospital, I was told that I had a punctured lung, several broken ribs and somewhat ironically, forty-six stitches.

Laying in that hospital bed, I had time to reflect. I remembered thinking of my wife, kids and grandkids while the truck was rolling. It was like slow motion and just like they say, my life passed before my eyes.

I wondered if I would ever see my precious family again. It made me realize just how much I loved them – and how much I value this life. Later, in my hospital bed, I had more time to reflect. I began to recall and really recognize the influence and life lessons that I learned from the woman that raised me…

My mother.

———

Dolores Plank is the person who has made the biggest difference in my life. I cannot remember her ever missing any of my games growing up. Football, basketball, baseball; it didn't matter. She was always there.

When I was at Ohio State, she tried to get to as many games as she could. She had suffered polio as a child and could not drive. That meant traveling over three hours on the bus or catching a ride. Whatever it took, she did everything possible to see my games.

As it turned out, I played in three Rose Bowls. But because we were a typical, blue-collar, Western Pennsylvania family, there just wasn't the money to get my mom out to California to those games. It was the Christmas season and most of my teammates' families traveled to the game. So for those three years, I played in those games with a heavy heart because the person that supported me most couldn't be there. So instead of having a big family celebration like my teammates, I carried on by myself. It was a lonely experience.

I vowed that if the opportunity ever came along, I was going to take my mother to the Rose Bowl. In 1997, Ohio State won the Big Ten and ended up playing against Arizona State in Pasadena. It worked out that I was able to take both parents to the Rose Bowl that year.

But my father had suffered two brain surgeries, and as you can imagine, it was difficult navigating through the thousands of people to get to our seats. So, we missed all of the pregame activities. Just moments after taking our seats, Ohio State took the field. The band was playing, people were cheering and I thought that this must be a moment of ecstasy for my parents.

I looked over at my mother and tears were running down her face. She was crying uncontrollably.

I said, "Mom, what's the matter? Are you okay?"

She said, "Doug, I wish I would have been here for you 25 years ago when you ran onto that field."

I was momentarily stunned. But then I looked at her and patted my chest.

I said, "Mom, you were. You were here; right here in my heart."

I will always remember that moment. You can kiss your family and loved ones good-bye and put miles between you, but at the same time, you can carry them with you in your heart and mind. After all, you don't just live in the world; the world lives in you.

———

You can see the power of influence that my mother had on me. Now it's your turn.

You now have the tools and mindset to begin from wherever you are today – and you can make a difference to yourself, to those around you – and perhaps even to those in the future.

You have learned that in order to make the last thing you ever do the greatest thing you ever do, you have to be unreasonable.

You have learned that it's the unreasonable and determined people who leave the greatest legacy.

You now also understand how to show up in the present moment of your life to suppress your survival instincts. It's those instincts that sometimes keep us confined to mediocrity because in fact, most situations in our daily lives are not about life and death survival. That's just our mind playing tricks and trying to keep us out of danger. You now know how to take charge of your mind.

You understand how to bring your "A" game. You now know how to push yourself harder with more energy. You now understand what it takes to always bring your best.

You understand the power of communication skills that help you and everyone around you be more successful and live better lives.

Perhaps most importantly, you understand the power of influence.

This is a power we all have.

I propose that today is the best day of your life to begin using your influence.

Why?

Because it's the one you've got.

Right now, in this moment:

What are you going to get done?

Your genetic potential is waiting.

Appendix A: VISION AND PLANNING EXERCISE

Reaching the upper limits of your genetic potential requires that you have a direction. A Vision and a Plan are critical components of any deliberate successful venture. Perform the steps below and remember, you are a player and not a spectator. That means actually performing the exercise!

1. People who underachieve typically have no plan. Beginning right now, ask yourself, "What is my vision for my future? Write it down. Dream big. Don't sell yourself short. As you will learn, you are more capable than you imagine.

2. Then ask, "What is my plan to attain this vision?" Beginning with the end in mind, work backwards and step by step outline what you need to do to achieve that vision. This plan will allow you to check your progress as you "follow the dots."

3. Next, put a deadline on the goals within your plan. Otherwise, your goals are simply wishes.

4. Again, commit to being a player and not a spectator. This will differentiate you from 80% of the population. Hoping and wishing without action produces nothing.

Appendix B: YOUR "A" GAME

Remember that your "A" game consists of:

- Attitude
- Aggression
- Anticipation
- Adversity: Adapt and Overcome
- Accountability
- Accomplishment

Review these "A" Game Questions daily:

What **attitude** will I choose for myself today?
What one to three tasks do I need to **aggressively** attack?
What might I **anticipate** could go wrong?
What will my behavior and attitude look like when **adversity** hits?
Who am I **accountable** to for the tasks I'm working on?
What do I need to have **accomplished** today for the day to have been a success?

Appendix C: The "46 Attack Mindset" Questions

In addition to your "A" Game questions, refer to these questions often to ensure continued personal and professional growth.

What are the three most critical items I need to get done today?
What's my plan of attack?
What roadblocks could keep me from achieving them?
What's my contingency plan in case these roadblocks occur?

What kind of physical exercise will I perform today? When will I execute that?

What is my eating/nutrition plan for today? When and what will I eat?

How will I make this day fun, productive and meaningful?

Whose day will I make today?
Who will I compliment and thank?
> How will I show "presence?" Can I remember to maintain an open, upright, expansive posture? Can I bring strong energy and a laser-like focus to the people I'm interacting with?

Remember:
1. Choose to be a player.
2. Choose your goal/target.
3. Create a plan.
4. Take aggressive action on your plan.
5. When adversity hits, adapt and use it to grow.
Repeat steps 1 through 4.

Appendix D: The 46 Bullet Point Summary

What if you approached every day as if you were on kickoff coverage? What if you aggressively attacked each day with the kind of energy and focus that a kickoff coverage requires?

This book provides a mindset and system that enables anyone to do just that.

Below are 46 bullet points to remind you of how to practice the "46 Attack Mindset" every day.

If you remember these points and practice these behaviors, you will begin to reach the upper limits of your genetic potential – and that's the most anyone can ask of a human being.

The "46 Attack Mindset" Bullet Points

1. Heroism comes from learning to suppress your survival instincts.
2. Reaching the upper limits of our genetic potential is to be the best we can be.
3. Don't wait to take action because eventually you are going to die.
4. Adopting the "46 Attack Mindset" can lead you to making the last thing you do the greatest thing you do.
5. The world's greatest accomplishments come from *determined* people.
6. We don't know what we're capable of until we take massive action.
7. Being proactive with positive action is always better than being reactive.
8. Make the choice to be a player as opposed to a spectator.
9. Focus on what you need to get done and not on what's going to happen to you.
10. There is going to be pain. But it's better to live with the pain of execution than the pain of regret.
11. Take initiative and act first in order to create opportunities.
12. Live aggressively and take advantage of the opportunities you create.
13. We are born fearless and then learn to be afraid.
14. Stay in the present moment and focus on what you need to get done in order to move through fear.
15. It's always about what you're going to do to them; it's never about what they're going to do to you.
16. The world is competitive and bringing your "A" game will propel you to success.

17. When you learn to control your mind, you can bring 100% intensity to all of your present moments.
18. Your "A" game consists of:

- Attitude
- Aggression
- Anticipation
- Adversity: Adapt and Overcome
- Accountability
- Accomplishment

19. When you choose to bring all of your mental and physical attention to the task at hand, you will bring results unlike you have ever previously produced.
20. Be a cause; not an effect.
21. Using anger appropriately can take you from mediocrity to excellence.
22. Create your vision and then implement the plan that will get you there.
23. See it, believe it and achieve it.
24. The ability to overcome adversity is the number one key to success.
25. Overcome the quitting conversation that keeps you from attaining your vision.
26. Not quitting is a trait available to all; it requires no skill – just will.
27. It's not how you start; it's how you finish. Be persistent.
28. Implement the 13 Elements of Control to take charge of what is in your power.
    a. How you show up each day
    b. How you look
    c. What you say
    d. How you listen to others
    e. What you eat and drink
    f. How often and how intelligently you exercise
    g. Your education and what you read and listen to
    h. The people who surround you
    i. The news you consume
    j. How you treat people and the success of your personal relationships
    k. How you spend your time
    l. Where you spend your time
    m. Your income, which is a direct result of the rewards you bring to others
29. Exploit matchups to put people in a position to win.
30. Communicate your message with an arrow straight to the heart; use emotion.
31. People don't care how much you know until they know how much you care.

32. If you tell people what to do; show them how to do it, and then empower them to go do it; your chances of success grow exponentially.
33. The words you use can either hurt or heal; use them wisely.
34. Hustle will always beat talent when talent does not hustle.
35. The ability to listen well is your number one communication skill along with the questions you ask.
36. To be a great speaker, be prepared, be comfortable, be committed, and be compelling.
37. Use presence, power and warmth to enhance your charisma.
38. Use the power of recognition and reward to influence behaviors.
39. Fire fast, hire slow.
40. Turn your life and your challenges into a fun, competitive game.
41. Strive to make your capabilities exceed your limitations.
42. Take a stand and design your character.
43. Tap into the awesome power of the human spirit because it is greater than any substance, temptation or obstacle you will face.
44. Identify your superpower; cultivate it and use it.
45. Use your power of influence. You never know the difference you might make.
46. Accept the challenge of making the last thing you ever do...the greatest thing you ever do.

SPECIAL BONUS APPENDIX E: SKILLS THAT DO NOT TAKE TALENT!

When I was at Ohio State, we were given rules to live by that would enhance both our athletic performance and our lives. They were called "Skills That Take No Talent." I immediately worked to incorporate these skills into my daily life. These are skills that are available to each of us, no matter who we are or what we do.

Not only did these skills make me a better athlete, they made me a better person. Think of the competitive advantage you could gain by taking these skills on until they become a part of you. I strongly encourage you to keep this list in front of you and each day, take a look at them to remind yourself of how you might improve yourself in these areas.

Here they are:

Concentration
Punctuality
Mental Toughness
Enthusiasm
Communication
Great Effort
No Missed Assignments
Awareness
Work with Speed
Execute Daily Responsibilities
Attitude
Maintain Good Social Habits
Patience
Toughness
Unselfishness
Finish

People ask me, "How do you get to the NFL?"

There are no shortcuts. There are no life hacks that get you to the top of professional sports just like there is no "one secret" that propels you to the top of the business world. It's a daily grind. But if you incorporate these "skills that take no talent" into your regular behavior patterns, you will establish a baseline of excellence that few people will be able to match.

These are the daily disciplines that will separate you from the pack. If you fall or have a setback, get back up, dust off and regroup. Ask yourself what you learned and how you can regain your momentum with improved effort and better focus. Every day brings a new opportunity. If others with less talent have achieved success, so can you.

ACKNOWLEDGEMENTS

No one achieves success by themselves. I met my wife, Nancy, at Ohio State when I accidently threw a snowball through her dormitory window. When I went to apologize, I knew I'd found the woman I'd spend the rest of my life with. Her love, support and unending patience have meant the world to me. She has been rock steady during all of the trials and tribulations that come with adult life, and I am so grateful to have her as my life partner. She has my enduring love, from now through eternity.

I also want to thank my mother, Dolores Plank, for her unending support and faith in my life long pursuits. I was only eight years old when she encouraged my brothers and me to compete in sports. She encouraged her three sons to participate in all sports as a method of understanding teamwork and learning the art of competition. In my case, it provided a college education and the opportunity to compete at a professional level. After suffering polio at the age of nine, she was never able to compete in sports or even drive a car. She wanted her children to experience things that she could not. By playing football, I was able to provide her the experience of being at the Rose Bowl, watching many Chicago Bear games at Soldier Field, and being at Ohio Stadium watching the Ohio State Buckeyes win every game at home during my Ohio State career.

DOUG PLANK BIOGRAPHY

Early life

Plank attended the Norwin School District in North Huntingdon, Pennsylvania where he participated in baseball, basketball, and football. His high school baseball batting average of .526 stood as a record for over 30 years. In his senior football season, he was voted MVP of the Foothills Conference in western Pennsylvania. He attended Ohio State University, winning three Big Ten titles and participating in three consecutive Rose Bowls under legendary coach Woody Hayes.

NFL playing career

In 1975, Plank was drafted by the Chicago Bears in the 12th round.

He spent his entire eight-year NFL playing career with the Bears. Plank was the first Bears rookie to lead the team in tackles. The only other rookie to accomplish that task since Plank was Brian Urlacher, a new member of the NFL Hall of Fame. Plank was a favorite of Bears defensive coordinator Buddy Ryan for his hard hitting and aggressive style, such that Ryan named his defense the "46 defense" after Plank's jersey number and his central position in the defense. Plank was considered one of the hardest hitting safeties in the game. That effort took a physical toll and he retired before the Bears reached their peak in 1985. Plank and Gary Fencik were dubbed "The Hit Men," a fact referenced by Fencik in 1985's The Super Bowl Shuffle. Plank was recently voted by ESPN Chicago as the fifth toughest Chicago Bear of all time. In addition, he was inducted into the Mike Ditka Gridiron Greats Hall of Fame in 2018.

After football

After football, Plank became a franchisee of the Burger King Corporation, operating multiple restaurants. In 1995 he began working as a football analyst and worked for Fox Sports, the Arizona Cardinals, the Arizona State Sun Devils, the University of Arizona Wildcats, and the Arizona Rattlers. In 1996, the "Bearman" became the unofficial mascot of the Chicago Bears, and he wears Plank's 46 jersey. Since 2001, Plank has worked as a football color analyst on national radio broadcasts for Sports USA Media and Westwood One. Until the current ranking system became effective in 2014, Plank was a voter in the weekly Harris Interactive College Football Poll, ranking the top 25 college football teams in the nation.

Coaching career

In 2001, Plank began his coaching career as a defensive coordinator in the Arena Football League. For three seasons, he worked under former Dallas quarterback Danny White. In those three seasons, the Arizona Rattlers played in three consecutive ArenaBowls. In 2004, Plank was hired by Arthur Blank to be head coach of the Georgia Force, an Arena Football team he owned in addition to the Atlanta Falcons. Plank was named the AFL's Coach of the Year in 2005 and 2007, leading Georgia to the playoffs in every season. In his first year, he led them to ArenaBowl XIX in 2005. In Plank's first four years as an AFL head coach, he won more games in that period than any other coach in the history of the AFL. In 2008, he was a seasonal assistant on the Atlanta Falcons staff. That year, the Falcons played in the Wild Card round of the NFL playoffs. In 2009 he served as the assistant defensive backfield coach for the New York Jets under head coach Rex Ryan, the son of Plank's former defensive coordinator, Buddy Ryan. The 2009 Jets defense led the NFL in fewest total yards allowed, fewest points allowed, and fewest TD passes allowed. That season, the Jets played in the AFC championship game versus the Colts. In 2010, Plank became a football program assistant at Ohio State. The Buckeyes earned a share of the Big 10 title with an 11–1 record and beat Arkansas in the Sugar Bowl. On August 31, 2011, Plank became head coach of the AFL's Philadelphia Soul. In Plank's first year, the Soul compiled a regular season record of 15–3 after going 6–12 the previous year. The Soul played in ArenaBowl XXV versus the Arizona Rattlers. The Soul established new franchise records in wins, scoring, rushing, and defensive takeaways in 2012. On September 5, 2012, Plank became head coach of the 4-14 Orlando Predators of the AFL. After losing the first five games of the 2013 season, Orlando rebounded to make the playoffs before losing in the first round. Plank then retired from coaching to pursue broadcasting and business opportunities.

Visit www.dougplank46.com

LEE WITT

Lee is an author, speaker, athlete, and musician with 30 years of experience in corporate communications. He lives with his wife, Brooke, in a Seattle suburb.

Visit www.leewitt.com

CPSIA information can be obtained
at www.ICGtesting.com
Printed in the USA
LVHW100707130221
679235LV00020B/159